The Glory of Man

OUR IDENTITY

Nancy!

I pray this will be a blessing to you, "Christ in you the hope of Glory." Colossians 1:27

David Bachook

The Glory of Man

OUR IDENTITY

DAVID BACHOROSKI

Flowing Streams Books
Colorado Springs, CO

The Glory of Man: Our Identity

Inquiries may be made to the author at:
bachord@aol.com

Published by Flowing Streams Books
www.flowingstreamsbooks.com

All scripture quotations are from the
New American Standard Bible (NASB), unless otherwise indicated.

The New American Standard Bible
Copyright © 1960, 1962, 1963, 1968, 1971, 1972, 1971, 1975, 1977, 1995 by The Lochman Foundation
Used by permission. www.Lockman.org

Scripture quotations taken from *The Amplified Bible*,
Copyright © 1954, 1958, 1962, 1964, 1965, 1987 by
The Lockman Foundation.
Used by permission. www.Lockman.org

Cover Design: Valerie Riviera-Dyer of StylePoint Design
Interior Design: Robert Dyer of StylePoint Design
Edited by: Robert Dyer of StylePoint Design
www.stylepointdesign.com

ISBN-13: 978-1-7312-0230-7
ISBN-10: 1-7312-0230-X

Printed in U.S.A.

DEDICATION

To my wife, Connie, for her love and encouragement as together we walk the path He has chosen for us to His Glory!

Table of Contents

INTRODUCTION

Since time began, man has sought what was lost. Thinking perhaps it could be found in education or philosophy, he attempted to attain all wisdom and knowledge, and discovered it was not there. Perhaps it could be found in science; he sought the answer to all mysteries and discovered it was not there. Ah! Maybe it could be found in politics, but after attaining the highest status among his peers he discovered it was not there either. Then he believed the answer was to be found in religion, so he did everything he could to climb the ladder to attain the lofty heights of heaven and discovered it was not there either. This thing that man lost is called glory. This book will show how it was lost and how it can once again be found.

PREFACE

The Race Official, seated at the registration table, eyed me as I walked towards him. "You don't look old enough to enter this race."

"I am, here's my driver's license."

Luckily in those days the driver's license didn't have your picture on it.

At the age of 15-years old I would steal my brother's driver's license, so I could race my buddy George's 1956 Corvette. I would race anything I could: hill climbs, road courses and gymkhanas. There was only one problem. I would win! I had to hide my trophies at George's parent's house, so my parents wouldn't find out. Needless to say, they would not have approved.

At that time there was nothing as exhilarating to me as racing. The need for speed got in my blood and I didn't worry about the dangers. I concentrated on the road. All my focus was right ahead of me. Nothing else mattered. While I was driving I knew when I had a good corner or a bad one. I don't think any driver has ever finished a race and said everything was perfect. There was always something I could have done better and faster, and it made me want to keep coming back.

I especially enjoyed hill climbs. It was just me against the mountain. When I would pull up to the starting line there would be hundreds of people lining the course ahead of me. I just wanted to do well. The engine would purr as it waited to go and do what it was made for. Somehow it knew that for this reason, it was made, and for this reason, if need be, it would die. My heart rate would begin to rise in anticipation of what was ahead. My hands would shake, and my mouth would be dry. Once the starter dropped the flag and I was on my own, everything would begin to calm down and I would retreat into my zone. This is the place where I was comfortable and at peace because I knew it so well; like coming home to an old friend. I could hear the roar of the engine; it would begin to scream as it was released from its captivity. The engine noise would be my guide. I knew when to shift by the sound of the engine. I would let it be my wild friend. I loved to hear it scream as it conquered the mountain. On every comer it would give me its approval to go faster and faster as it scratched and clawed its way up the mountain. When we would reach the finish line it smelled of burning oil and was bleeding from antifreeze boiling over. The car was a mess. The tire treads were gone, and tires were worn out from clawing their way up the mountain. The brakes smelled from too much heat and were barely useable, but it was happy. It seemingly did its job to the best of its ability. Whether we won or not, I knew the car and I had been one, if even for a short time. I would try to catch my breath and wait for my time to be announced. No matter what the time, I won. For just a moment in time I falsely believed that I had conquered the mountain. Hmmm! I wonder. Could this be glory?

Since cars were a big part of my life, I worked as a custodian at the GM Pikes Peak Test Headquarters after school. I knew I wanted to test cars. I got in my 1962 Corvair and drove from Colorado Springs to Milford, Michigan, where the General Motors Proving Ground was located. I pulled up to the entrance of the Proving Ground and was directed by the guard to the employment office. After doing all the paperwork I met with Swanny, the person who gave the tests. He said, "I know that you can drive because you drove here from Colorado Springs. I'm going to take you to a corner on the track and see how good you are. If you can pass this test I will hire you." We went on the track to the East/West Straightaway. At the end of the straight section of the track was a banked corner that you couldn't take if you were going under 60 MPH. This was to turn you around to go in the opposite direction. That corner was so steep that you couldn't even stand on it without falling off.

He took the corner and said, "Now can you do that?"

I said, "Sure."

I'd never seen a road like that before, but I knew I had to do it. On the first try, I did it.

"That's great," he sounded impressed. "However, there is just one problem."

"What's that?"

"You're only twenty years old, we've never hired anyone that young to be a test car driver. If you can get your parents to sign a permission letter, we'll hire you."

I called my parents, got them to sign a permission letter, and I was hired as the youngest driver they ever had at the Proving Ground. Hmmm! I wonder, could this be glory?

Although it was fun testing cars to their max, after a while I became bored, and began seeking something more. They offered me a permanent job in Michigan, with an option of returning to Colorado Springs where I might be hired on full time. I chose to return to Colorado Springs and worked again at the Pikes Peak Test Headquarters while going to business college and taking mechanic courses. In 1969 the boss retired, and I was offered the position of Manager of the GM Pikes Peak Vehicle Test Headquarters. That is where I worked until, after five thousand trips up the Pikes Peak Highway, and 33 years of working for General Motors, I retired in 1999. During my career I received much glory from man. The best part was I was called by God and became a born-again Christian in 1972, along with my wife. I never thought I would find anything as exciting and fulfilling as my life had already been. But I found the excitement of living the Christian life far exceeded, and continues to exceed, anything that had gone before.

I had attended church all my life. I was taught the word of God and knew the historical Jesus. However, I had no relationship with the personal Jesus. During my time of wandering in the desert I was a choir director at our church. I knew all the right words and phrases and even became involved in the occult until the Lord was gracious enough to allow me to have a personal relationship with Jesus Christ. I found that I was seeking information, but the Lord wanted to give me revelation. During my time in church I heard the pastor speak of glory. We knew that all glory should go to the Lord. All things were to be done to His glory, but I didn't realize what that meant. I thought I had glory. The pastor said we were created for His glory. Why would I want something that I thought I already had? I knew, or thought I knew and experienced this glory, the glory of man. Eventually I began to understand this quest was just beginning. I needed, somehow, to understand the glory of God and what it means in contrast or in conjunction with the glory of man.

The Glory of Man
Section One

Glory Defined

The Glory of Man

The study of Glory is fascinating. You could even say it's glorious!

GLORY DEFINED

Glory. The very word is packed full of meaning. In the contemporary sense, we tend to think of it in terms of honor, distinction or esteem.

A nation's heroes are often its founders, who received wide acclaim due to their heroic efforts in battle, exploration, discovery, or courageous confrontations defying great odds. One thinks of Alexander the Great, George Washington, Christopher Columbus, Lewis and Clarke, just to name a few.

In the sports world most would agree that inspiring figures with names like Pele, Mantle, Unser, Spitz, Armstrong and Phelps have received, or in some cases lost their glory.

The special distinction of glory extends to the arts, whether it concerns renowned paintings like DaVinci's Mona Lisa, or grand statues such as Michelangelo's David. It also includes varieties and styles of music, stage productions, literary masterpieces, poems, and yes, supremely produced, and usually well financed films. The point is, we know glory when we see it. What these incomplete lists illustrate is the glory we both see and ascribe to the people involved in talented and creative endeavors.

Yet there is more:

When speaking of the glory of man it has much to do with the root word, (dokeo) which is the root word of, (doxa) glory.

17

Dokeo means to think or suppose, according to *The Complete Word Study Dictionary*, [1] written by Spiros Zodhiates. "The word primarily means thought or opinion, especially favorable human opinion, and thus in a secondary sense reputation, praise, honor (true and false), splendor, light, perfection, rewards (temporal and eternal). Thus, the doxeo of man is human opinion, and is shifty, uncertain, often based on error, and its pursuit for its own safety is unworthy."

Donald Gray Barnhouse writes in *Romans Volume II*, "If the glory of man is honor, esteem, praise, reputation and an estimate of genuine and merited worth, the glory of God is honor, esteem, praise, reputation and estimate of the genuine and merited worth of God.

The most common Greek word translated glory is doxa. It has come down to us in our word doxology. How it got to mean glory, praise and honor is an interesting study. Hundreds of years before Christ, there was a word commonly used in Greece which means *to seem, to appear*. The noun of the words came to mean *an opinion*, which is the way a matter appears or seems to one person. This word for opinion has given to us such words as paradox (strange opinion), orthodox (straight opinion), and heterodox (other opinion). Little by little the word began to be used for an opinion of a person, whether a good opinion or a bad opinion, and finally in the Bible it began to be used for a good opinion only. From there on, it came to mean praise, honor and glory resulting from the good opinion." [2]

There are many times when the Lord showed the manifestation of His divine presence, His glory, through wrath, death and destruction. Think of the deliverance of Israel from the bondage of Egypt, when Israel crossed through the Red Sea and the waters returned and killed the Egyptian army, or the awesome presence of God on Mt. Sinai, when the earth trembled and shook. The destruction of Sodom and Gomorrah, when the walls of Jericho fell down and gave Israel the victory over their enemies. When David killed Goliath and delivered Israel from the hand of the Philistines. Shadrach, Meshach and

Abednego in the fiery furnace. Daniel's deliverance from the lion's den. The wrath of God poured out on the Lord Jesus Christ as payment for our sin.

We can see this in our own day, when against all odds Israel once again became a nation, and against all odds the United States and its allies prevailed in World War II. As the hand of God was upon Israel so the hand of God was upon the free world for His glory. "He delivered us from the hand of our enemies that we might serve Him without fear." Luke 1:74

> *When darkness surrounds us when our enemies arise, whom shall we fear? You alone Lord are our light and our salvation. How shall we then be moved? Will You not, great Father of Glory, rise up on our behalf? Will you not, as in days of old, cause Your voice to be heard? Will you not show the lightning down your arm? Will you not with indignation and anger, with the flame of a devouring fire scatter our enemies? We will call upon You, trusting not in our own merits, Lord, but in the merits, in the authority of our love scarred redeemer. Of whom then shall we be afraid? (Prayer by John Hayes)*

"Men who had the right opinion of God were able to form a correct estimate of His greatness and majesty. Hence, they began to consider more and more the attributes of God which He has revealed: His power, majesty, love, greatness, loving-kindness, tender mercies, goodness, and His perfections without end. Therefore, little by little the word for 'opinion,' which became the opinion about God, came to include praise of God for all that He is and for all that He thinks and does.

"The Anglo-Saxon word which competed with the word *glory* for a time is our word *worth*. When we think of the worth of God we are thinking of the glory of God. And when we praise Him, we are acknowledging His worth, and are therefore engaged in the contemplation of His *worthship*. Now as worth-ship was hard to pronounce, the difficult letters were dropped in the course of time and our noun *worship* is the result. There is no difference in meaning between the worship of God, the praise and adoration of God and the glory of God." [3] Worship is ascribing glory and worth to God.

His glory and His worth has been expressed in many songs and hymns using such words as: Majestic, Awesome, Beautiful, Good, Glorious, Radiant, Pure, Light, Sovereign, Almighty, Holy, Faithful, Wonderful. Of course, the English language, like any language, is bankrupt and destitute when speaking of His glory and worth.

We have seen politicians and soldiers in the news who have lost their glory and honor in an instant. Man's glory is changeable and is not trustworthy. Even un-regenerate man hates it when men lie, cheat, murder, and do not display the attributes of God. "For many walk, of whom I often told you, and now tell you even weeping, that they are enemies of the cross of Christ whose end is destruction, whose god is their appetite, and whose glory is in their shame, who set their minds on earthly things." Philippians 3:18-19 "But My people have changed their glory for that which does not profit." Jeremiah 2:11 "The glory of man is as the flower of grass. The grass withers and the flower falls off." 1 Peter 1:24. In contrast the glory of God is absolutely true and changeless. Are you worshiping God to get a blessing from Him or are you worshiping Him because He is the blessing?

God's opinion marks the true value of things as they appear to the eternal mind, and God's favorable opinion is true glory. This contrast is shown in John 5:44 "How can you believe, when you receive glory from one another, and you do not seek the glory, *favorable opinion,* that is from the one and only God?"

GLORY DISPLAYED

The true glory or worth of man is the ideal condition in which God created man. This ideal condition was lost in the fall, spiritual death, and is recovered through the work of Jesus Christ.

Genesis 1:26 - 27 says, "Let us make man in our image, after our likeness, and let them have dominion over the fish of the sea, and over the fowl of the air, and over the cattle, and over all the earth, and over every creeping thing that creepeth upon the earth. And God created man in His own image, in the image of God He created him, male and female He created them."

"Then the LORD God formed man of dust from the ground, and breathed into his nostrils the breath of life; and man became a living being." Genesis 2:7

If I make a sculpture of a lion, the sculpture is not the substance. It is not really a lion. It is the image of a lion. In order to have a likeness there has to be a true. The sculpture simply reflects the true. When man was created in the image of God, man was not the substance, he was the image created to reflect the truth about God. In the beginning Adam reflected the true image and character of God. When God looked upon Adam, He saw Himself. The glory of man was God himself. The glory of God ascribes honor and admiration, dignity and splendor, praise and applause, infinite perfection, divine majesty and holiness, excellence and splendor.

Man was created to reflect the image of God, His character and worth. Man was not the substance. He was the image. Man was not created to reflect the image of the angels, but to reflect the image of God. "I am the LORD, that is My name; I will not give My glory to another, nor My praise to graven images." Isaiah 42:8 "Everyone who is called by My name, and whom I have created for My glory, whom I have formed, even whom I have made." Isaiah 43:7 "Has a nation changed gods when they were not gods? But My people have changed their glory for that which does not profit." Jeremiah 2:11

When Jesus humbled himself and came to earth as sinless man the scriptures say: "He is the radiance of His glory and the exact representation of His nature, and upholds all things by the word of His power." Hebrews 1:3 The Amplified Bible puts it this way: "He is the sole expression of the glory of God — the Light-being, the out-raying of the divine — and He is the perfect imprint and very image of (God's) nature, upholding and maintaining and guiding and propelling the universe by His mighty word of power."

Psalm 8: 3-6 "When I consider thy heavens, the work of thy fingers, the moon and the stars, which thou hast ordained; what is man, that thou dost take thought of him? And the son of man, that thou dost care for him? Yet thou hast made him a little lower than God, (Elohim), and dost crown him with *Glory* and majesty! Thou dost make him to rule over the works of thy hands; Thou hast put all things under his feet." (New American Standard Version.)

The angels were watching as God formed this new thing on the earth. The angels asked, "What is man?"

"What is a man?"

One of the angels, peeking behind a tree, may have asked his friend; "What is it?"

"I don't know, but I heard God call him Adam, which means red."

"Where did He get it?"

"He made it, he was formed from the dust of the earth, and there certainly is a lot of red dirt around here."

"Can we call him 'Big Red?'"

"I don't think so; God wanted him to be called Adam."

"What is it for?"

"I think he was formed to reflect God's image."

"I know he's not God but he certainly looks like God."

"He's awesome! As I look at him I can better see what God is like."

"I think he was created to rule and have dominion over the earth!"

"Yeah! I think you're right."

Man was crowned with Glory. Man was not crowned with diamonds, gold or rubies. These were things that were destined to perish. Man was crowned with God's Glory! The Glory of God is God Himself. Glory is the manifestation of the presence of God.

GLORY LOST

In time past, Satan was dethroned from heaven and cast down to earth.

Isaiah 14: 12-14 "How you have fallen from heaven, O star of the morning, son of the dawn! You have been cut down to the earth, You who have weakened the nations! But you said in your heart, I will ascend to heaven; I will raise my throne above the stars of God, and I will sit on the mount of assembly in the recesses of the north. I will ascend above the heights of the clouds; I will make myself like the Most High."

Satan saw that his power was now being usurped by man. If he could tempt man and get him to disobey God, then man would lose his covering of Glory and his dominion over the earth. If he could defeat man and get him to disobey God, he would have forever defeated God. Man was given a free will and could choose to obey or disobey God, and he chose to disobey. When Adam sinned, the Glory of God departed; this is known as spiritual death.

Genesis 3:8-10 "And they heard the voice of the Lord God walking in the garden in the cool of the day: and Adam and his wife hid themselves from the presence of the Lord God amongst the trees of the garden. And the Lord God called unto him, where art thou? And he said, I heard Thy voice in the garden, and I was afraid, because I was naked; and I hid myself."

The covering of Glory that Adam had was gone. Fear came into his life and he saw that he was naked.

"For in Adam all die." 1 Corinthians 15:22

Let's say that you are taking a hike in the mountains of Colorado with a few friends, and you come onto a very deep gorge that is 100 feet wide that you need to get across to get to your destination. One of your friends was a track star in high school, who did the long jump. He thinks he can jump across the gorge, so he makes a run for it. He makes it about 20 feet, but he comes up short and crashes on the rocks below. Another friend was a pole vaulter, so he gets his pole and jumps about thirty feet, but still comes up short and crashes on the rocks below. You were a rock climber and know how to climb down one side and back up the other side. You get your climbing gear, but discover the gorge is deeper than you thought, and the rope is not long enough. After making an attempt you too crash on the rocks below. You were all sincere, tried hard and believed in what you were doing. But you still came up short. In a similar way we have all come short of the glory of God. Our intentions might be good. We might try hard, but we still come up short. The goal is beyond our reach. Of course, the gap that separates us from being all that we were created to be is our sin.

There are times when we choose to sin, and we expect to be punished, but I assure you it's much worse than that. We come short of His glory.

"For all have sinned and come short of the Glory of God." Romans 3:23

If you're playing with your kids in the park and one of them falls and hurts himself, your immediate reaction is to run to the child, hold him in your arms and comfort him. God could not do that. If He would have touched Adam, His Glory would have consumed him. "For our God is a consuming fire." Hebrews 12:29 He consumes sin.

God spoke that man would have dominion over the works of His hands. Psalm 8:6 God's Word will always come to pass. He cannot lie. Here was a dilemma. How could man have dominion over the works of His hands without the Glory of God? Satan thought he had won, but God had a plan from eternity. He would restore the Glory that was lost. He would bring life back into man, exactly what dead men need.

From all eternity there was a redemption plan for man. There was no redemption plan for the angels that had fallen, so Satan thought that he had won. He thought he had forever defeated God. This is very aptly expressed in the song written in 1894 by Johnson Oatman, Jr.

Holy, Holy, Is What The Angels Sing

Refrain: Holy, Holy is what the angels sing,
And I expect to help them make the courts of heaven ring.
But when I sing redemption's story, they will fold their wings,
for angels never felt the joys that our salvation brings.

But I hear another anthem, blending voices clear and strong,
"Unto Him who has redeemed us and hath bought us," is the song;
We have come through tribulation to the land so fair and bright,
In the fountain freely flowing He has made our garments white.

Then the angels stand and listen for they cannot join the song,
Like the sound of many waters, by that happy, blood washed throng,
For they sing about great trials, battles fought and vict'ries won,
And they praise their great redeemer, who hath said to them, "Well done."

So, although I'm not an angel, yet I know that over there
I will join a blessed chorus that the angels cannot share;
I will sing about my Savior, who upon dark Calvary
Freely pardoned my transgressions, died to set a sinner free.

If Satan had seen the plan, he never would have allowed God's spotless lamb to be lifted to the altar of the cross, where His innocent blood could be shed to cleanse man, and to pay the price so once again man could stand in the Glory of God's presence.

1 Corinthians 2:7-8 "But we speak the wisdom of God in a mystery, even the hidden wisdom, which God ordained before the world unto our glory; which none of the princes of this world knew; for had they known it, they would not have crucified the Lord of Glory."

These things were hidden for us, they were not hidden from us. When you hid your children's Easter eggs they were hidden in such a way that they could be found, not so they would never be found. In the same way the mysteries of God were hidden in such a way that they could be found by those who seek Him. "Ask, and it will be given to you; seek, and you will find; knock, and it will be opened to you. For everyone who asks receives, and he who seeks finds, and to him who knocks it will be opened." Matthew 7:7-8

GLORY RESTORED

The glory that man lost in Adam has been restored in the second Adam, Jesus Christ. "The last Adam became a life-giving spirit." 1 Corinthians 15:45 The glory that was lost can only be found in Him. We are glorified in Him as we allow Him to be glorified in us.

Jesus, who was God, is God and always will be God, became man. Adam was formed in the image of God. Jesus who was the essence of God was made in the image of man. While on earth some things He did as our example, other things He did as our substitute. Everything He did on earth, He did in total dependence on the Father, as man. In our day we hear people ask, "What's normal?" Jesus was the only normal person to ever walk this earth. He lived on earth as God intended man to live.

"Have this attitude in yourselves which was also in Christ Jesus, who, although He existed in the form of God, did not regard equality with God a thing to be grasped, but emptied Himself, taking the form of a bond-servant, and being made in the likeness of men. And being found in appearance as a man, He humbled Himself by becoming obedient to the point of death, even death on a cross." Philippians 2:6-8

Jesus said in John 5:19, "Truly, truly, I say to you, the Son can do nothing of Himself, unless it is something He sees the Father doing; for whatever the Father does, these things the Son also does in like manner."

And again, in John 14:10 "Do you not believe that I am in the Father, and the Father is in Me? The words that I say to you I do not speak on My own initiative, but the Father abiding in Me does His works."

And further in John 5:30 Jesus said, "I can do nothing on My own initiative. As I hear, I judge; and My judgment is just, because I do not seek My own will, but the will of Him who sent Me."

The disciples recognized this and spoke of this in Acts 2:22, "Men of Israel, listen to these words: Jesus the Nazarene, a man attested to you by God with miracles and wonders and signs which *God performed through Him* in your midst, just as you yourselves know."

Jesus walked in total dependence on the Father and we are to walk in total dependence on Him. "So Jesus said to them, Peace be with you; as the Father has sent Me, I also send you." John 20:21

"And He died for all, so that they who live might no longer live for themselves, but for Him who died and rose again on their behalf." 2 Corinthians 5:15

"The mystery which has been hidden from the past ages and generations; but has now been manifested to His saints, to whom God willed to make known what is the riches of the glory of this mystery among the gentiles, which is Christ in you, the hope of Glory." Colossians 1:26-27

"For it was fitting for Him, for Whom are all things, and through Him are all things, in bringing many sons to glory." Hebrews 2:10

"And all of us, as with unveiled face, (because we) continued to behold (in the Word of God) as in a mirror the glory of the Lord, are constantly being transfigured into His very own image in ever increasing splendor and from one degree of glory to another; (for this comes) from the Lord (Who is) the Spirit." 2 Corinthians 3:18 Amplified Bible

Salvation is not only what we *are saved from* — the devil and sin — resulting in death.

Salvation is also what we *are saved to* — God and His Glory! — resulting in life.

It is the Blood of Jesus that *cleanses* us (sanctification), and *covers* us (justification), and *enables* us to stand once again in His Glory (redemption).

Jesus prayed to the Father in John 17:4-5 and said, "I glorified Thee on the earth, having accomplished the work which Thou hast given me to do. And now, Glorify Thou Me together with Thyself, Father, with the Glory which I ever had with Thee before the world was." "And the Glory which Thou hast given Me, I have given to them; that they may be one, just as We are one." John 17:22

"Father, I desire that they also, whom Thou hast given Me, be with Me where I am, in order that they may behold My Glory, which Thou hast given Me; For Thou didst love Me before the foundation of the world." John 17: 24

"Worthy is the Lamb that was slain to receive power and riches and wisdom and might and honor and glory and blessing. And every created thing which is in heaven and on the earth and under the earth and on the sea, and all things in them I heard saying. "To Him who sits on the throne, and to the Lamb, be blessing and honor and glory and dominion forever and ever." Revelation 5:12-13

GLORY IN THE CHURCH

The church may be described as the body of believers which is filled with the presence, power, agency and riches of God in Christ.

Man was created to express the truth about God

One of the ways that God has chosen to display His glory today is through His church, the Body of Christ. Although many have turned His church into an organization it is really an organism. The church universal is a gathering of believers where each member is humbly allowing Jesus Christ to live His life through them. As this is done the manifestation of the presence of God, His character and His worth, is displayed on the earth through His people. God has His people everywhere. I've been at many prayer meetings where people have prayed to see His glory manifested. Open your eyes and just look around you; at His people.

In our churches today, it can no longer be business as usual. We have been put on display so the whole world can come and see what God is like. Are they disappointed or are their hopes and dreams fulfilled? More importantly, we need to ask: Is God disappointed? Are His hopes and dreams fulfilled? "Christ loved the church and gave Himself up for her; that He might sanctify her, having cleansed her by the washing of water with the word, that He might present to Himself the church in all her glory, having no spot or wrinkle or any such thing; but that she should be holy and blameless." Ephesians 5:25-27 Hmm! I wonder; has He set His expectations too high for us? Or maybe, just maybe, we have set our expectations too low and are willing to accept the status quo and business as usual. The military has a slogan. "Be all that you can be, join the Army." Do I dare say; be all that you can be, join His church.

"I pray that the eyes of your heart may be enlightened, so that you may know what is the hope of His calling, what are the riches of the Glory of *His inheritance* in the saints." Ephesians 1:18

When Jesus died He left the Father an inheritance: it was us.

There are times in scripture where the word *glory* isn't used but expresses the same idea. For instance, Paul in his letter to the Ephesians calls it the *fullness of God.*

"For this reason I bow my knees before the Father, from whom every family in heaven and on earth derives its name, that He would grant you, according to the riches of His glory, to be strengthened with power through His Spirit in the inner man, so that Christ may dwell in your hearts through faith; and that you, being rooted and grounded in love, may be able to comprehend with all the saints what is the breadth and length and height and depth, and to know the love of Christ which surpasses knowledge, that you may be filled up to all the fullness of God." Ephesians 3:14-19

I was saved, I am being saved, and one of these days I will be saved. In the same way; I was given His glory, I am being changed into His glory and one of these days I will receive the fullness of His glory. A day is coming when we will be allowed to share in all the fullness of His Glory, but not now.

Many times today the manifestation of the presence of God is like the wind. You can't see the wind, but you can see the effects of it when it is moving. This is especially evident when a sinner, bound for hell, repents and receives eternal life. That is more impressive than any other manifestation of the presence of God.

"For now we see in a mirror dimly, but then face to face; now I know in part, but then I will know fully just as I also have been fully known." 1 Corinthians 13:12

Ever since Adam sinned man has yearned to be clothed with the Glory Adam had at the beginning. We long to be clothed with God Himself.

"For we know that if the earthly tent which is our house is torn down, we have a building from God, a house not made with hands, eternal in the heavens. For indeed in this house we groan, longing to be clothed with our dwelling from heaven, inasmuch as we, having put it on, will not be found naked. For indeed while we are in this tent, we groan, being burdened, because we do not want to be unclothed but to be clothed, so that what is mortal will be swallowed up by life." 2 Corinthians 5:1-4

This is expressed in the final verse of the hymn:

The Old Rugged Cross

To the old rugged cross, I will ever be true,
Its shame and reproach gladly bear;
Then He'll call me some day
To my home far away,
Where His glory forever I'll share.

"Therefore, I exhort the elders among you, as your fellow-elder and witness of the sufferings of Christ, and a partaker of the Glory that is to be revealed," 1 Peter 5:1

"...The Lord Jesus Christ; who will transform the body of our humble state into conformity with the body of His Glory, by the exertion of His power that He has even to subject all things to himself." Philippians 3: 20-21

"When the Chief Shepherd appears, you will receive the unfading crown of Glory." 1 Peter 5:4

GLORY IN HIS PEOPLE

The true glory of man is the manifestation of the Divine Presence of God in him.

"But Thou, O Lord, art a shield about me, my glory, and the one who lifts my head." Psalms 3:3

First Corinthians 12:4-6 speaks about *effects* in the New American Standard Bible which says, "Now there are varieties of gifts, but the same Spirit. And there are varieties of ministries, and the same Lord. And there are varieties of *effects*, but the same God who works all things in all persons."

If you've been a Christian for any time at all, you know and have studied the gifts of the Spirit as spoken of in 1st Corinthians 12: 8-10, and Romans 12. These are not an all-inclusive listing of the gifts of the Spirit because others are spoken of in various other passages in the New Testament. 1st Corinthians 12:6 speaks of *effects* (NASB), *diversities of operations* (KJV) *different kinds of workings* (NIV) and *distinctive varieties of operation* (Amplified).

The word *effects* is defined in Strong's Concordance as, (1755) *energema*, thing wrought; effect, operation, and workings. These things are not necessarily commonly referred to as the gifts of the Spirit but are important workings of God in the body of Christ.

King David had his mighty men who were given extraordinary skill in battle as spoken of in 2 Samuel 23:8-9. One of his men, Adimo the Eznite, killed 800 men at one time. Another man, Benaiah, went down and killed a lion in the middle of a pit on a snowy day. 2 Samuel 23:20 Abishai killed 300 men with a spear. 2 Samuel 23:18. These mighty workings of God are not necessarily what we would call the gifts of the Spirit, but they were amazing and extraordinary works of God to bless Israel.

When King Solomon set out to build the temple in Jerusalem Huram, the king of Tyre said in 2 Chronicles 2:13-14, "And now I am sending a skilled man, endowed with understanding, Huramabi, the son of a Danite woman and a Tyrian father, who knows how to work in gold, silver, bronze, iron, stone and wood, and in purple, violet, linen and crimson fabrics, and who knows how to make all kinds of engravings and to execute any design which may be assigned to him, to work with your skilled men, and with those of my lord David your father." This man Huramabi, who had much wisdom and knowledge, could not have gone to school long enough to know how to work with all those things. Each one could take a lifetime of study. The Lord gave him those skills and understanding, and he also had to know how to act as foreman to work with the experts in those various fields. Not only was Huramabi skilled, but Solomon was blessed with discretion and understanding as spoken of in 1 Chronicles 2:12. These special effects or diversities of operations are spoken of everywhere in the Old and New Testament. We could speak of Sampson, Noah, Joshua, Peter and Paul and others whom the Lord used to do great things. These were just ordinary people devoted to God. The people weren't great, the works of God were great in those people, therefore, we call them great. What made them great was that they were obedient and faithful to what God had called them to do.

In the body of Christ today the works of God are just as prevalent as they were in Bible times, we just haven't recognized them. "There are varieties of effects, but the same God who works all things in *all persons*. But to *each one* is given the manifestation of the Spirit for the common good." 1 Corinthians 12:6-7 These gifts, ministries and effects are not given just to the special chosen few, but they are *given to all*, to be *used by all*, for the common good as He chooses to glorify the Lord Jesus Christ.

The word *energema*, holds a clue to what God is doing through you. The base word is where we get our word *energy*. What has God given you the energy to do? What turns you on?

Whatever it is, God can use it to bring glory to the Lord Jesus Christ through you. "For it is God who is at work in you, both to will and to work for His good pleasure." Philippians 2:13 "Whether, then, you eat or drink or whatever you do, do all to the glory of God." 1 Corinthians 10:31 "And whatever you do in word or deed, do all in the name of the Lord Jesus, giving thanks through Him to God the Father." Colossians 3:17. I encourage you to be you, as God intended you to be. Expect Him to do great things through you, not because you're great, but because He's great and He has chosen to work in this world through you. It is important that, especially in these last days, "the whole body, being fitted and held together by that which every joint supplies, according to the proper working of each individual part, causes the growth of the body for the building up of itself in love." Ephesians 4:16 Just because I'm not a toe doesn't mean that I don't need a toe.

It has been said that, "Glory is the manifestation of the presence of God." As God works through you, you are displaying the manifestation of His presence in this world. In the parable of the minas in Luke 19:13 KJV the Lord said to "occupy" until I come. To occupy is your occupation, it is what the Lord has called you to do, this is your ministry. The NASB says "do business," that which keeps you busy is your ministry in the body of Christ. God has His people everywhere, because God wants to work everywhere. The benefits we receive from God are not given to us as wages. His blessings cannot be earned by our efforts. In Christ we are not in an employee/ employer relationship. We are in a father/son relationship. The son serves in loving obedience as he can. The Father gives as He wills. We are not owners of God's gifts, we are stewards of the gifts He has entrusted to us. Whether we are a pint, quart or gallon makes no difference. In Christ we are all full. Each one is given all it can hold. The pint is just as full as the gallon. By comparison one is bigger than the other, but by experience each is full. He will fill you with all that you can hold, and as He does we are each completely satisfied in Him. If you want more of Him, give Him more of yourself. "As each one has received a special gift, employ it in serving one another as good stewards of the manifold grace of God." 1 Peter 4:10 However, I warn you, do not become puffed up. You're not special, the gift is special. The only thing that makes us special, is that we are in Christ. "You are my servant, Israel in whom I will show my glory." Isaiah 49:3

Even though God has given each of us natural talents and abilities to carry out His work, He still doesn't want us to do it without Him. He wants to be a part of everything we do because we can't do it without Him.

Thank you, Great God, for the incredible array of saints portrayed in Your magnificent book. We see in them both spiritual attractiveness, and fleshly blemishes. Everywhere we look, they're saddled with the same passions and infirmities as we. Even the most renowned among them faltered in their worst moments, they fell. You picked them up from the dust and the dunghill...you cleaned them up, set their feet upon a rock, and established their goings. In their greatest moments, it was Your hand that sustained them... You made your strength perfect in their weakness... They triumphed neither in their might nor power but in Yours...You are as You were...ever present in times of need. We are as they were...insufficient and dependent. Thank you that we need You always... that You are always there and that just as the Bible depicts...victory, always comes through You. (Prayer by John Hayes)

SHEKINAH GLORY

What is this thing that causes the strongest man to fall on his face and the weakest among us to rise above the clouds? It is what makes the lame to walk and the blind to see, gives hope to the desperate and courage to the feeble, makes kings to bow their knee and emperors to sulk in shame. It is the magnificent Shekinah Glory of God. He can turn darkness to light simply by His Presence.

The inner glory of God has an outward manifestation. The original Greek word was used to translate a Hebrew word *shekinah* which has given the word glory a second meaning. This Hebrew word means *splendor* and *brightness*. The Talmud speaks of the Shekinah glory. The word shekinah is not in the Bible. The shekinah can be described as the visible physical manifestation of the presence of God, or that which is detected by one or more of our five physical senses. In many places in the Bible it can be seen, but not called shekinah. There is a physical manifestation of the presence of God:

- as seen in creation — Genesis 1:2
- at the burning bush — Exodus 3:2
- in the plagues in Egypt — Exodus 9:14
- in the pillars of cloud and fire in the wilderness — Exodus 13:21
- with Moses coming down from Mt. Sinai — Exodus 34:29
- in the cloud of Glory at the temple dedication — Exodus 40:35

It is further seen:
- at the birth of Christ when the shepherds saw the glory and the angels announced the birth of Jesus — Luke 2:9
- at Jesus baptism — Luke 3:22
- on the mount of transfiguration — Matthew 17:2
- at the crucifixion — Matthew 27:52
- at His resurrection — Luke 24:4
- at the death of Stephen — Acts 7:55
- and at the outpouring of the Holy Spirit on the day of Pentecost — Acts 2:2-3.

These were all physical manifestations of the Divine Presence of God. Some of these manifestations were not only what people saw with their eyes, but also what they heard with their ears. The voice of God was heard:
- at Mt. Sinai — Deuteronomy 5:25
- at His birth — Luke 2:9

- at His baptism — Matthew 3:16-17
- at the Mount of Transfiguration — Matthew 17:5
- and among many other times and places.

When Moses spent time in the presence of God on Mount Sinai, he came down from the mountain and the glory of God was manifested on him. The glory did not come from him. He was reflecting the glory of being in the presence of God. "It came about when Moses was coming down from Mount Sinai (and the two tablets of the testimony were in Moses' hand as he was coming down from the mountain), that Moses did not know that the skin of his face shone because of his speaking with Him." Exodus 34:29

Many physical manifestations of God's presence were also seen in the numerous miracles that God did through Jesus and the followers of Jesus. "Men of Israel, hear these words: Jesus of Nazareth, a Man attested by God to you by miracles, wonders, and signs *which God did* through Him in your midst, as you yourselves also know." Acts 2:22 Miracles are manifestations of the presence of God that can be seen with our eyes, heard with our ears or felt with our senses. "Jesus said to her, 'Did I not say to you that if you would believe you would see the glory?'" John 11:40

Today one of the most evident displays of the physical manifestation of the presence of God can be seen with our eyes in His creation. The Apostle Paul speaks of this in Romans 1:19-23 "...that which is known about God is evident within them; for God made it evident to them. For since the creation of the world His invisible attributes, His eternal power and Divine nature, have been clearly seen, being understood through what was made so that they are without excuse. For even though they knew God, they did not honor Him as God, or give thanks; but they became futile in their speculations and their foolish heart was darkened. Professing to be wise they became fools, and exchanged the glory of the incorruptible God for an image in the form of corruptible man and of birds and four-footed animals and crawling creatures."

There are those who can see His glory expressed in His creation and they begin worshiping His creation instead of Him who is the creator. The creation displays the handiwork of God not His substance. The creation of God is not to be worshiped. It is to be used (not abused) and enjoyed but not worshiped. If you think the creation is really something you should look at the magnificence of the creator.

But even His earthly creation, as glorious as it is, was tarnished in the fall. "For the anxious longing of the creation waits eagerly for the revealing of the sons of God. For the creation was subjected to futility, not willingly, but because of Him who subjected it, in hope that the creation itself also will be set free from its slavery to corruption into the freedom of the glory of the children of God. For we know that the whole creation groans and suffers the pains of childbirth together until now. And not only this, but also we ourselves, having the first fruits of the Spirit, even we ourselves groan within ourselves, waiting eagerly for our adoption as sons, the redemption of our body." Romans 8:19-23

"For you will go out with joy and be led forth with peace; the mountains and the hills will break forth into shouts of joy before you, and all the trees of the field will clap their hands." Isaiah 55:12

My wife and I were driving out of Denver to the west and as we came over a hill we could see the clouds wisping over the majestic snowcapped mountains she said, "Isn't that beautiful?" And I said: "Yes, it's glorious."

"The heavens are telling of the glory of God; and their expanse is declaring the work of His hands." Psalm 19:1

"There are also heavenly bodies and earthly bodies, but the glory of the heavenly is one, and the glory of the earthly is another. There is one glory of the sun, and another glory of the moon, and another glory of the stars; for star differs from star in glory." 1 Corinthians 15:40-41

The creation is not the glory of God. The creation reflects the glory of God.

COUNTERFEIT GLORY

In dealing with the study of God's word we invariably need to deal with counterfeits. The Glory of God has many counterfeits in this world. The enemy will always try to counterfeit that which is valuable and true. You will never see a counterfeit paper bag because it is not worth counterfeiting. The simple fact that there is a counterfeit proves that there is a true.

"...the god of this world has blinded the minds of the unbelieving, that they might not see the light of the gospel of the glory of Christ, who is the image of God." 2 Corinthians 4:4

Many cults, isms, and churches attempt to display the attributes of God without the Divine Presence of God. The enemy's main goal is to get you to trust in anything or anybody other than the person of the Lord Jesus Christ.

Man was created in the image of God and now fallen man attempts to create god in the image of fallen man. "The fruit of the Spirit of God is love, joy, peace, patience, kindness, goodness, faithfulness, gentleness, self-control." Galatians 5:22 These are attributes of God produced by the Spirit of God in the lives of a born-again child of God. These attributes of the divine presence of God can be, and are, counterfeited. Many in this world are seeking the peace of God in all the wrong places. His peace can only be found in Him. He is the Prince of Peace.

Many today ascribe supreme glory and worth to things other than God. There are those who get tricked into worshipping wealth, position, power and fame. They bow down to the things in the world instead of the One who gave them those things. "They worshipped and served the creature instead of the creator, who is blessed forever." Romans 1:25

There are times when Christians get caught up in wanting all that God can give them instead of wanting God Himself.

"All of God is available to the man who is available to all there is of God." – Ian Thomas. The glory of God is the manifestation of the divine presence of God. "Seek Him and you will find Him if you search for Him with all your heart." Jeremiah 29:13 We cannot afford to become distracted in our day. The true glory of man is the manifestation of the presence of God in him.

DISTRACTIONS TO GLORY

You've heard about distracted drivers and the accidents they've caused. Drivers are distracted by cell phone usage, text messaging, passengers, and even bugs flying around the inside of the car. In our day many in the church are being distracted from its real mission of, "Go ye therefore and preach the gospel." Mark 16:15. The church is called to be a light in a dark place.

After many years of attending Bible Studies and Prayer Meetings, I've noticed a tendency towards turning to the things of this world instead of sticking to the main purpose. What I mean by that is a tendency towards emphasizing the deeds of darkness instead of our victory in Christ. There is no end to the things we can speak or pray against. It usually begins with the statement, "The problem in this world is...," and then we go on emphasizing such things as our president, our government, our schools, or our economy. The list goes on and on. It all sounds very pious and spiritual, but it is a waste of time and effort. We are in danger of becoming distracted and having a wreck.

This is not to say that we should not be aware of the pitfalls and darkness of this world, but we should not become preoccupied with them. There are those in the body of Christ who are called by God to warn the church of such dangers and may God bless them in their ministry to us. However, we need not focus on these things because the worries of this world will choke the word and it becomes unfruitful. "And the one on whom seed was sown among the thorns, this is the man who hears the word, and the worry of the world, and the deceitfulness of riches choke the word, and it becomes unfruitful." Matthew 13:22

At the Lord's first coming, the world was darkness and He came into the darkness to bring light. He did not wait until the world was light before He came. "Those who walk in darkness have seen a great light." Isaiah 9:2, Matthew 4:16 He came so that those who were in darkness would not remain in darkness. "I have come as light into the world, that everyone who believes in Me may not remain in darkness." John 12:46

When you go home late at night and you walk into a dark house, do you begin yelling and hollering at the darkness or do you turn on the light? You, of course, turn on the light and the darkness goes away. In this world we can either holler or complain about the darkness or we can turn on the light. The darkness cannot overpower the light. The darkness must flee. If the light is on in your kitchen late at night and you open your back door, the darkness cannot come creeping into your kitchen. In the natural world the darkness cannot overpower the light, it is much truer in the spiritual world.

Did you ever wonder why, when a church is praying for revival the darkness is exposed? We've all heard about the dark deeds of pastors and teachers being exposed. The news media loves to tell the stories. When the Spirit of God begins to work, as He answers prayer for revival, the darkness is exposed as the Light comes in. Much of this exposure is proof that God has heard your prayers and is working to produce revival. Sometimes Christians like to quote Ephesians 5:11 to justify exposing and gossiping about the darkness, but they quote only the part of the passage that says to expose them, but we are told to expose them to the light. "And do not participate in the unfruitful deeds of darkness, but instead even expose them; for it is disgraceful even to speak of the things which are done by them in secret. But all things become visible when they are exposed by the light, for everything that becomes visible is light." When the light shines, darkness is exposed. If you want to expose the darkness, send the light.

Revival is an act of God, going into this dark world and bringing light. We can go into this dark world and talk about the darkness, holler at it, curse it, or we can be among those who are used by God to bring light into this dark world. Second Corinthians 4:6 says, "For God, who said, 'Light shall shine out of darkness,' is the One who has shone in our hearts to give the light of the knowledge of the glory of God in the face of Christ."

First Corinthians 4:5 says, "Do not go on passing judgment before the time, but wait until the Lord comes who will both bring to light the things hidden in the darkness and disclose the motive of men's hearts." In his book, *The Harbinger*, Johnathan Cahn is quoted as saying; "If the righteous had been the lights' they were called to be, our nation would never have fallen." [4] Somehow, we feel that if we pray against the darkness the light will automatically come. That is not true. The Lord warned about this in the story about when the enemy is cast out in Luke 11:24-26, "When the unclean spirit goes out of a man, it passes through waterless places seeking rest, and not finding any, it says, 'I will return to my house from which I came,' And when it comes, it finds it swept and put in order. Then it goes and takes along seven other spirits more evil than itself, and they go in and live there; and the last state of that man becomes worse than the first."

Just because the darkness is cast out does not automatically mean the light has come in. Light is not the absence of darkness, light is the presence of God. "The light shineth in darkness; and the darkness comprehended it not." John 1:5 The Amplified Bible says it this way, "And the Light shines on in the darkness, for the darkness has never overpowered it — put it out, or has not absorbed it, has not appropriated it, and is unreceptive to it."

One of our biggest causes of our focusing on the distractions is fear. Jesus came into the darkness to bring light. Jesus was not afraid of the dark and we should not be afraid of the dark either. We are the ones who are, "...protected by the power of God through faith for a salvation ready to be revealed in the last time." 1Peter 1:5 I heard it quoted, "The problem in this world is not the presence of darkness, it is the absence of light." The purpose of revival is to usher in the light of the presence of God. If you're not safe in the lion's den with Jesus you're not safe anywhere.

The church was built on the strong foundation of God's Word, Prayer, Praise and Worship. It will continue to stand if the foundation stays strong. If the foundation develops a crack, you fix it. If the foundation is allowed to crumble, the entire building comes down. The various ministries of the church can only stand if the foundation of prayer, praise and worship stays strong. Although the foundation of a building is not visible and does not receive praise it is the most important part of any building. Every part of the building functions only if the foundation supports it.

When Nehemiah was given the task of rebuilding the walls at Jerusalem he remained steadfast and completed his task. If he would have become distracted and started tearing down the walls of his enemies, the wall at Jerusalem would never have been rebuilt. If he would have wasted his time on tearing down the walls of his enemies the only result would have been more torn down walls. The walls of Jerusalem would have remained torn down. In the church, whenever our wall is attacked we automatically think that we need to go and attack the enemies' walls instead of repairing the crack in our own wall. This is often another distraction of the enemy to keep us from completing our task.

• • •

We cannot afford to become distracted by warring against symptoms. We need to go after the source of the symptoms. The enemy's goal is to steal, kill and destroy. John 10:10 "For our struggle is not against flesh and blood, but against the rulers, against the world forces of this darkness, against the spiritual forces of wickedness in the heavenly places." Ephesians 6:12 When we begin calling flesh and blood the enemy, we have taken our eyes off the main foe and we have fallen right into Satan's trap. Satan does not care what kind of attention he gets, as long as he gets attention. He's just like a spoiled child. All he wants is attention, good or bad, he doesn't care. I refuse to give him the attention he does not deserve. My attention should be focused on the Lord Jesus Christ. "But I am afraid, lest as the serpent deceived Eve by his craftiness, your minds should be led astray from the simplicity and purity of devotion to Christ." 2 Corinthians 11:3

We cannot become distracted by warring against symptoms. Our President is not the problem, he is a symptom of the problem. Homosexuality is not the problem, it is a symptom of the problem. Abortion is not the problem, it is a symptom of the problem. There is no end to talking about the symptoms in this country or any other. Don't waste my time talking about the symptoms. We have been called to a much higher calling than that. This country needs a Revival. We are not to sit and be distracted by a bunch of symptoms. You don't put a Band-Aid on a broken arm. You go after the root, not the symptoms. We are called to, "Encourage the exhausted, and strengthen the feeble. Say to those with palpating heart, take courage, fear not." Isaiah 35:3-4

Somehow, we think that talking about the problems will eliminate the problems — no it only makes them stronger. The Lord catches His fish, and then He cleans them. We need to focus on bringing people into the Kingdom of God and then let the Lord clean them up.

Do not become distracted by what other believers are called to do. What they are doing might be good. It's what God has called them to do. Every part of the body needs to be focused on what God has called them to do, not what He's called others to do. Be aware, but not distracted. We cannot be all things to all people, only Jesus is capable of that.

What shall we then do? One response is explained in the parable of the tares in Matthew 13:27-30 "And the slaves of the landowner came and said to him, 'Sir, did you not sow good seed in your field? How then does it have tares?' And he said to them, 'an enemy has done this!' And the slaves said to him, 'Do you want us, then, to go and gather them up?' But he said, 'No; lest while you are gathering up the tares, you may root up the wheat with them. Allow both to grow together until the harvest; and in the time of the harvest I will say to the reapers, first gather up the tares; and bind them in bundles to burn them up; but gather the wheat into my barn.'"

The wheat is very precious to the Lord and He does not want us to do anything that would damage it, including pulling up the tares. That is not our job. One big example of this is shown by the apostle Paul while he was in prison in Rome. You may have noticed in the epistles that Paul never bad-mouthed the Romans, their leadership or what horrible things they were doing to Christians. He told us to pray for those who are in authority. First Timothy 2:1-2 Although he lived in one of the most ungodly times and in a place where persecution of Christians was commonplace, Paul had every opportunity to talk bad about the government, but he didn't. It was not the job he was sent to do. For most of us, it's not part of our job description either. People everywhere love to talk about the problems. If I wanted to talk about everything that is bad about this country, or world, I could go to any local coffee shop on any given morning, and that is all I would hear people talk about. Only we have the answer to the problems, and that answer is the Lord Jesus Christ and prayer.

We know that when we pray according to God's will He hears our prayers. We also know that when we ask the Lord to bless someone or something He will go to work on their behalf. We also know that the Lord is a gentle shepherd who will not push His way into places where He is not wanted. The Lord does not mind going into a dark place to bring light. We know of certain people, organizations or government entities that will not invite the Lord into their situation. We, however, as Christians can give the Lord the invitation to bless our government, our President, our schools and every dark institution with His presence. When you pray and invite the Lord into their lives, He will honor your prayers and He will go. That is not saying that they will automatically change, but they will be given the opportunity to change. Remember, He can change darkness to light simply by His presence. Many times, He does not have to do anything, but simply be there. His presence alone will change things.

Many times, events are like a boat on an ocean. There are times when we pray, it is like a speed boat that turns as soon as we turn the wheel. And other times it is like turning an ocean liner. It begins turning as soon as the Captain turns the wheel, but it may not look like it for a long time. As long as the wheel is held, and pressure is applied it is turning, whether we see it or not. I urge you to continue praying, keep the pressure applied. It is turning, and God is working whether you see the evidence or not.

SPECIAL GIFTS IN THE BODY

Is it possible that our view of the "Church" is much too small?

Does your gathering of believers constitute the Church?

Does your congregation constitute the Church?

Does your particular denomination constitute the Church?

When Paul wrote to the churches of Galatia he did not write to one local gathering of believers. The churches he is referring to is the entire Roman province including the cities of Antioch, Iconium, Lystra and Derbe in the southern province. He could also be referring to the cities in the northern province including Phrygia, Pisidia, Lycaonia, and Isauria.

Romans 12:4-5 "For just as we have many members in one body and all the members do not have the same function, so we, who are many are one body in Christ, and individually members one of another."

This is an interesting project: I challenge you to read 1 Corinthians 12 as referring to the entire body of Christ, not just your local congregation. Also read Ephesians chapter four with the same thing in mind.

Billy Graham was called to be an evangelist. Was he an evangelist only to the Baptists or to the entire body of Christ? There is not a Christian denomination that has not been touched by his ministry. This is a good illustration of the body of Christ working together. Imagine the impact we would have on the world if the entire body was working together as it should in unity.

If each church or denomination were complete in itself, they would not need the other parts of the body. We have not yet received all that God wants to give us until we receive what God wants to give us through other believers.

45

"And the glory which Thou has given Me I have given to them; that they may be one, just as We are one. I in them and Thou in Me, that they may be perfected in unity, that the world may know that Thou didst send me, and didst love them, even as Thou didst love Me." John 17:22-23

There are some today in the body of Christ who believe they have some special gift, power or ability from God that is not available to other Christians. They believe that they are unique and special to the body of Christ. This is not so. That way of thinking promotes egotism, pride and arrogance. As a born-again Christian you have no more gifts, powers or abilities than is available to any born again Christian who is devoted to God, in the body of Christ, as He chooses. You are not special; the gift is special. Handle with care.

You may have a unique ministry in the body of Christ. The Lord can use that as He chooses. But you, individually, in yourself, have no special power or gift. The power is of God. The ability is of God, and the gifts are of God. "There are varieties of gifts, ministries and effects given by God who works all things in *all persons.* To *each one* is given the *manifestation of the Spirit* for the *common good.*" 1 Corinthians 12:4-7 These gifts, ministries and effects were not given to the special chosen few, but to all to be used by all for the common good as He chooses. There is no system of superiority or inferiority: all are equal in Christ. "But from those who were of high reputation, what they were makes no difference to me, God shows no partiality." Galatians 2:6 Paul said, "In no respect was I inferior to the most eminent apostles, even though I am a nobody." 2 Corinthians 12:11 Jesus is Lord; but he will not lord it over you. If you have a bad appendix you go to the hospital and have an appendectomy to remove the infected appendix. Our churches need a *religiostomy* to remove the infecting religious spirit from our churches.

In the church, "All things must be done properly and in an orderly manner." 1 Corinthians 14:40 In the local church there are certain tasks that need to be done. Not everyone has been called to count the offering or to preach. There are people appointed to certain ministries and each one must be done well to complete the whole. However, promoting a hierarchy in the church encourages pride and arrogance. Jesus vehemently opposed this in the book of Revelation when He opposed the teaching of the Nicolaitans. Revelation 2:15 In your church whose ministry is the most important? The most important ministry is the ministry of the Lord Jesus Christ as He works through us, we are simply servants of Christ. We are not sent here to build up our own kingdoms, but the Kingdom of God. You cannot have a kingdom without a king, Jesus is the King. Your ministry must not draw attention to yourself, but to the Lord Jesus Christ. It must not be done in such a way as to cause a show to glorify yourself. It is not the activity that makes something good or bad, it is the origin of the activity.

Suppose that your pastor goes out to his car on a Sunday morning to drive to the church and speak before hundreds of people, and his car won't start. Whose ministry is more important then, the pastors' ministry or the mechanic? What if people came to your church on a Sunday morning and the sidewalks were covered with ice and the restrooms were so dirty that people would leave? Whose ministry is more important at that time the elders or the custodian? In an orchestra whose ministry is the most important the clarinet or the violin? Each individual part is incomplete without the whole working together to produce a beautiful sound. Every part of the body needs the other parts of the body. Just because I'm not a foot doesn't mean that I don't need a foot.

No Christian is an island unto himself. You are part of the body of Christ and need to put yourself under the authority and subjection of a local church or body of believers. If a part of the body is going off doing its own thing in total disregard to the other parts of the body, it is called cancer and will cause destruction to the rest of the body. It must be eradicated. This is for your own protection. If you have a campfire and take out one burning stick it will soon go out without the support of the rest. When a wolf is going after the weakest member of a herd, he will first separate the weakest member from the herd and then destroy him. Who are you in subjection to? Are you part of the body or are you doing your own thing. You must be subject to correction in order to grow. Do not allow yourselves to become offended when you are corrected. Becoming offended will choke the word. Mark 4:16-17 in the Amplified Bible says: "And in the same way the ones sown upon stony ground are those who, when they hear the Word, at once receive it with joy; and they have no real root in themselves, and so they endure for a little while, then when trouble or persecution arises on account of the word, they immediately are *offended — become displeased, indignant, resentful*; and they stumble and fall away." Being offended will choke the word; the word will choke these things.

When I was drawn into the occult, (in my case Transcendental Meditation) forty years ago, I was seeking God and I was, not knowingly, vulnerable to the ways of the enemy. One very common tactic of the enemy is to say:

"If you want to be closer to God you need to _____." and fill in the blank.

Or "If you want to be all that God wants you to be you need to let me _____." and again fill in the blank.

These statements should immediately raise a red flag. These people claim to have some special gift or power from God and need you to bow to their power and authority. None of the prophets or apostles in the Bible ever worked that way, and God does not work that way today. Be assured, "your adversary, the devil prowls about like a roaring lion, seeking someone to devour." 1 Peter 5:8 But he does not appear like a roaring lion, "Satan disguises himself as an angel of light." 2 Corinthians 11:14 "Such men are false apostles, deceitful workers, disguising themselves as apostles of Christ." 2 Corinthians 11:13. It took three years of delving into the Word to be delivered from the effects of TM. My wife and I could not watch TV, read a magazine or anything other than the Word of God. I know that you will find this hard to believe, but there were times when we would turn on the TV, sit down on the couch, and the Lord would turn it off. He wanted us into His Word. We would study many times up to twenty hours a day. Oh, the wonderful cleansing power of God's Word. One important thing I learned through all of this was: if it's not from God, I don't want it. I had to learn the value of contentment.

CONTENTMENT

Webster's defines "discontentment" as — restless aspiration for improvement.

Webster's Dictionary defines "contentment" - as to limit oneself in requirements, desires or actions.

The Greek word for "content" is *arkeo*, and gives the idea of *raising a barrier*, be content, be enough, suffice and to be sufficient.

The Amplified Bible expresses this very well in Hebrews 13:5-6 "Let your character or moral disposition be free from love of money– (including) greed, avarice, lust and craving for earthly possessions-and be satisfied with your present (circumstances and with what you have): for He (God) Himself has said, I will not in any way fail you nor give you up nor leave you without support. (I will) not in any degree leave you helpless, nor forsake nor let (you) down, (relax My hold on you). –Assuredly not! So, we take comfort and are encouraged and confidently and boldly say, The Lord is my Helper, I will not be seized with alarm–I will not fear or dread or be terrified. What can man do to me?"

Circumstances cannot make you content. "I have learned to be content in whatever circumstances I am." Philippians 4:11

Things can't make you content, "If only I had this or that I would be content." Contentment comes from trusting the Lord.

"Do not fret or have any anxiety about anything, but in every circumstance and in everything by prayer and petition (definite requests) with thanksgiving continue to make your wants known to God. And God's peace (be yours, that tranquil state of a soul assured of its salvation through Christ, and so fearing nothing from God and content with its earthly lot of whatever sort that is, that peace) which transcends all understanding, shall garrison and mount guard over your hearts and minds in Christ Jesus." Philippians 4:6-7 Amplified Bible

There comes a time when I need to say, "I must raise a barrier, I am content, I am satisfied and say that is enough, I am thankful." If it's not from God, I don't want it! "Godliness with contentment is great gain." 1 Timothy 6:6 NKJV

Heavenly Father, "Keep deception and lies far from me, give me neither poverty nor riches; feed me with the food that is my portion, lest I be full and deny Thee and say, 'Who is the Lord?' or lest I be in want and steal, and profane the name of my God." Proverbs 30:8-9 Amen.

• • •

You are not to build your theology on one passage taken out of context. Your theology basis must be taught in the Old Testament, New Testament, Gospels and the Epistles. If what you are doing deals with ego and pride and promotes arrogance it does not glorify the Lord Jesus Christ. It is akin to dealing in witchcraft. Love builds up, knowledge puffs up. 1 Corinthians 8:1 says "Knowledge makes arrogant, but love edifies." "In Him you have been made complete." Colossians 2:10 You don't need someone to give you some special gift to make you complete in Christ. You are already complete in Christ.

When speaking of the work of the Holy Spirit the Lord said; "He shall glorify Me, for He shall take of mine, and shall disclose it to you." John 16:14 The purpose of the Holy Spirit is to glorify the Lord Jesus Christ, not to glorify himself or the gifts, but the person of the Lord Jesus Christ. I urge you therefore to "humble yourselves, therefore, under the mighty hand of God, that He may exalt you at the proper time." 1 Peter 5:6 "I am afraid, lest as the serpent deceived Eve by his craftiness, your minds should be led astray from the simplicity and purity of devotion to Christ." 2 Corinthians 11:3

When the Bible speaks of gifts, the emphasis is on equipping for service, not imparting something free. Spiritual gifts are active and functional rather than passive. We are not owners of God's gifts; we are stewards of the gifts He has entrusted to us.

Lord with Your Word, You not only reveal and teach us eternal truth but...You speak to us personally! How precious are Your words to us...How tenderly and intimately You woo each one of us through lovely pages of life...You encourage and reprove us...You give us guidance and instruction. How great Your tender mercies dear God. To think...that we who earned torment and devastation...we who were stiff-necked and rebellious...we who were Your enemies and did not want You to rule over us are forgiven, cleansed, and welcomed into Your royal family...You love us so that You have brought us into the very bosom of the One whom most of us spurned...the Glorious Son of Righteousness...Thank you for your promises! Thank You for Your faithfulness to fulfill them... Thank You for speaking to us through Your Word. Thank You for Jesus...Thank You for saving us...How bountifully You have blessed us. (Prayer by John Hayes)

ARMOR OF GLORY

Can you imagine what it would be like to go to war while being totally unprepared? If you have been a Christian even for a short time, I'm sure you've discovered we have an enemy that wants to destroy us. The Lord said, "The thief comes only to steal, and kill and destroy, I came that they might have life, and might have it abundantly." John 10:10

As a prayer warrior it's important to be properly equipped. We need to have the right armor to go to war. "For though we walk in the flesh, we do not war according to the flesh, for the weapons of our warfare are not of the flesh, but divinely powerful for the destruction of fortresses. We are destroying speculations and every lofty thing raised up against the knowledge of God, and we are taking every thought captive to the obedience of Christ." 2 Corinthians 10:3-5.

Before you put on His armor we need to take off our own. The armor of God isn't added to what we have; it is to take the place of what we have. "Put off anger, wrath, malice, slander, and abusive speech from your mouth. Do not lie to one another, since you laid aside the old self with its evil practices, and have put on the new self who is being renewed to a true knowledge according to the image of the One who created him." Colossians 3:8-10

"Now the deeds of the flesh are evident, which are; immorality, impurity, sensuality, idolatry, sorcery, enmities, strife, jealousy, outbursts of anger, disputes, dissensions, factions, envying, drunkenness, carousing, and things like these, of which I forewarn you just as I have forewarned you, that those who practice such things shall not inherit the kingdom of God." Galatians 5:19-21 "For out of the heart come evil thoughts, murders, adulteries, fornications, thefts, false witness, slanders. These are the things which defile the man." Matthew 15:19-20 These things show us how bad our hearts are, and only Jesus has the power to change a person's heart. You might change your mind about some things, but only He can change your heart. He is in the heart changing business.

"Knowing this that our old self was crucified with Him that our body of sin might be done away with, that we should no longer be slaves to sin; for he who has died is freed from sin." Romans 6:6 "Even so consider yourselves to be dead to sin, but alive to God in Christ Jesus." Romans 6:11

One definition of flesh is that which we can see, touch, hear, taste or smell. It is that which is governed by our five physical senses. Another word used for flesh is *carnal*. An easy way to remember that is, when you order chili con-carne it is chili with meat. God became incarnate and dwelt among us. "And the Word became flesh and dwelt among us." John 1:14. We've all heard of a person who is carnal. He trusts only in what he can see, touch, hear, taste or smell.

During the days of yore, King Arthur had his Knights of the Round Table. Each had their own special armor. Sir Lancelot would put on his armor and you would say: "Oh look, here comes Sir Lancelot." You would recognize him because of his armor. Anyone who put on Sir Lancelot's armor would be mistaken for Sir Lancelot. We are told to put on the armor of God. As we go to war we are to put on the right armor, "The armor of God." Ephesians chapter six has much to say about the armor. One thing I know is this: as you live life, battles are going to happen; you will experience difficult times, and it is important to prepare for the battle before the battle comes. Don't wait to prepare for the battle after the enemy has attacked; prepare now so that when the attack comes you will be strong and will be able to walk through it in His strength and power. "Put on the full armor of God, that you may be able to stand firm against the schemes of the devil." Ephesians 6:11.

We are told to gird our loins with truth, (His truth), put on the breastplate of righteousness, (His righteousness) shod your feet with the preparation of the Gospel of Peace, (His Gospel — His Peace) shield of faith, (His Faith) helmet of salvation, (His salvation) sword of the Spirit, which is the word of God, (His Word).

Put on the armor of God not by effort, but by rest. We put on the armor of God by resting in the finished work of Jesus Christ. "For we who have believed enter that rest..." Hebrews 4:3 "For the one who has entered His rest has himself also rested from his works, as God did from His." Hebrews 4:10.

God's word prepares you for war. It shows you what you have received in Christ Jesus. "You are my war club, my weapon of war." Jeremiah 51:20.

Thank you so, Lord for crucifying our old man with Christ so that the body of sin might be destroyed. You command us to put him off. Therefore, by faith I do put him off. I likewise, reject vile words, lying, blasphemy, malice, wrath, and all the imaginations and high-minded things of my flesh in Jesus' name. Holy Spirit, deliver me from my own ways, decrease me, and prune the fruitless things from my life so that Jesus can be evidenced in and through me.

Thank you, God, for the cross of Christ, whereby I'm delivered from the lust of the eyes, the lust of the flesh, the love and cares of the world, idolatry, pride, arrogance, haughtiness of spirit, presumption, self-exaltation, vanity, guile, an independent attitude, vain imaginings, and every-thing that glorifies anything other than Him. By faith, in His triumphant name, I cast down such things; take every thought captive to his obedience; and lay aside the sin that so easily besets me.

In obedience to Paul's command, and by faith, I now put on my new man, our Lord Jesus Christ, bowels of mercies, kindness, meekness, humbleness of mind, long suffering, forbearance, forgiveness, and love the bond of perfect-ness. Lord, increase, glorify, and reveal my Savior in me this day. Manifest through me His holiness, and gentleness, His lowliness of mind, and the fear of God. I submit to His yoke and take it upon me; I repudiate my inclination to lean upon my own understanding. Grant me, instead, Spirit of Truth; the understanding which You give and enable me to lean entirely upon Jesus. (prayer by John Hayes)

GLORY EXPECTATIONS

Major W. Ian Thomas gave an illustration that is worth contemplating, and I paraphrase: Let's just suppose that there are aliens off somewhere in the universe; and they heard, through the celestial grapevine that on Earth God had created a man in His own image. Since they had never seen God they were very enthused to go to Earth and by seeing man they would know what God was like. They ready their spaceship and after a long journey they touch down on planet Earth in a large vacant lot in the middle of a big city.

Through their observance of Earth people, they discover that God is a drunk and he gossips and is only interested in his own wellbeing. They walk into a tavern where a television is playing the daily news program and they hear about terrorist bombings and murder and corruption in government. They discover that men not only kill each other but even their own offspring. They ask a patron of the bar; "Where would I go to find what God is like?" The patron lifts his head off the table and points across the street to a church building. They leave the tavern and walk into the cold dark building. There are some people there, but they discover that they are arguing about some unknown theological question. They discover others that won't even look at them and overhear them talking about the bad thing going on in their church. They are completely ignored. On their way out of the church one of them picks up a dusty old book and takes it with them.

After becoming completely disillusioned on their quest to discover what God was like they couldn't wait to return to their spaceship and leave planet Earth.

GLORY EXPRESSED

There are those in the church who have a religious spirit. They worship the church instead of the One to whom the church should be pointing. There are those who put their trust in the scriptures instead of the One to whom the scriptures are pointing. When talking to the Pharisees Jesus said, "You search the Scriptures because you think that in them you have eternal life; it is these that testify about Me; and you are unwilling to come to Me so that you may have life." John 5:39 There are those who are guilty of trusting in their prayers instead of the One to whom they are praying. The glory is not the church, the glory is Christ who is in the church.

Do you believe that it would be unreasonable to go to a gas station and expect to buy gasoline for your car? How many times would you continue to go to the same gas station that had no gasoline to sell? It wouldn't be long, and you would stop going to that particular station. In the same way we ask people to attend our church and they will find God. What if they come and find the divine presence of God is not there? How many times would you expect them to return? Are they being unreasonable in their expectations? Would you be surprised if God showed up at your church?

The glory of God could not be hidden but showed on the face of Moses when he came down from the mountain after being in the presence of God. In a similar way it shows when you are walking in the presence of God in your daily walk.

I heard of a missionary couple who were walking down the street in Tel Aviv, Israel. A woman approached them and asked; "Where did you get that peace?"

I was in a restaurant in Manitou Springs, Colorado and a young woman came to my table and said: "You convict me of my sin!" If you are walking in the presence of God, you can't hide it. "His glory shall be seen upon thee." Isaiah 60:2 KJV

As Moses turned aside to look at the burning bush, there wasn't anything special about that bush, any old bush will do as long as it is set apart, (sanctified) for God's use. Jesus rode into Jerusalem on a donkey that had never been ridden. As people shouted, sang praises and waved palm branches, did the donkey think it was about him? The only thing special about that donkey was that he was set apart, (sanctified) for the Master's use.

I worked for years as a mechanic and there were certain tools that I enjoyed using. They were comfortable in my hand. I knew that if I used a particular tool I could trust it to do the job that I asked it to do. It wouldn't fall short of the task, neither would it go beyond what I asked it to do.

In a similar way God has His toolbox of born again believers. When He has a task to be done He will go to His toolbox and choose a tool that is comfortable in His hand, one He can trust and one that won't go beyond what He asks of it. God has deliberately limited Himself and has chosen to do His work on the earth through His sons and daughters. You've heard it said, "If God wanted that done He would have done it Himself." That is not true, He has graciously chosen to do His work through His people. "He has committed to us the word of reconciliation." 2 Corinthians 5:19

A while back I was driving to a prayer meeting and I was praying about the meeting when I heard the Lord say: "Tell

Pastor Diana that I trust her." She was a tool that God knew He could trust to do His work, His way, to His glory.

Years ago, the Lord told my wife and I to go to Arizona and stay at Andy and Judy's house for a week. These were dear friends of ours, but they were not born-again Christians. I called them and asked if we could stay at their house for a week. They welcomed us and were eager to have us come. I told my daughters we were going to Arizona to stay at Andy and Judy's house for a week. They asked,

"Why are you going?"

"Because the Lord told us to." I said.

"What are you going to do while you're there?" they asked.

"I don't know, we were just told to go." I said.

During the week we loved them, as we spent all day, every day discussing and answering their questions about God. Toward the end of the week, God was so gracious. He drew them to accept Jesus Christ into their lives. They are both now strong pillars in their church.

I am so humbled to think that God trusted us enough to be used to do His work. Sure, there were Christians in Arizona who could have done the job, but He was gracious to allow us to be used of Him. We learned that time, distance or money are of no consequence when the Lord has a job to be done through His people, for His glory.

The bush didn't do anything special; it just burned. The donkey didn't do anything special; he just allowed Jesus to get on his back and he walked. We are to simply allow God to live in us and through us as He desires; we need to simply yield ourselves to Him and watch Him burn.

There have been those in leadership positions in the church who underestimate the power of God's glory in their lives. They minister to people in need, and because of ego and pride falsely believe, the persons they are ministering to are attracted to them instead of the Christ who is in them. Ministers, the same as anybody else, can easily get trapped and fall into various sins if they do not keep their eyes on the Lord. In our day there is so much talk about rights. *You have no right to do what God forbids.*

The Glory of Man
Section Two

Glory by Faith

GLORY BY FAITH

We need to take a look at what Jesus did to restore the Glory that was lost. We know that the answer is to be found in the person of the Lord Jesus Christ as the Holy Spirit reveals Him to us. "He shall glorify Me, for He shall take of mine, and shall disclose it to you." John 16:14 We need to look at two words: the Blood and Baptism.

The following became true over 2,000 years ago. They will not become true to you until you count them as true in your daily experience. Paul uses the word *reckon*. As you grow in Christ, the Holy Spirit will *quicken* or make to come alive these things in your life. As you meditate on these things, think of how you would act if these things were true in your daily experience.

THE BLOOD

"For the life of the flesh is in the blood, and I have given it to you on the altar to make atonement for your souls; for it is the blood by reason of the life that makes atonement." Leviticus 17:11 This passage has been called the John 3:16 of the Old Testament. "For as for the life of all flesh, its blood is identified with its life." Leviticus 17:14

"Is not the cup of blessing which we bless a sharing in the blood of Christ? Is not the bread which we break a sharing in the body of Christ?" 1st Corinthians 10:16

The blood of Christ not only symbolizes the death of Christ, but also the life of Christ. He poured out His life, so we could share His life in us. He took the punishment of our sins for us that He might live His life in and through us. "And the testimony is this: "God has given us eternal life, and this life is in His Son." 1st John 5:11

In communion, when we take the blood, we should remember His sacrifice to the Father as payment for our sin, as our substitute. We should also remember, He died in our stead that we might share His life. Praise Him for His love and grace.

We were redeemed by His blood:

"Be on guard for yourselves and for all the flock, among which the Holy Spirit has made you overseers, to shepherd the church of God which He purchased with His own blood." Acts 20:28

"In Him we have redemption through His blood, the forgiveness of our trespasses, according to the riches of His grace." Ephesians 1:7

"...knowing that you were not redeemed with perishable things like silver or gold from your futile way of life inherited from your forefathers, but with precious blood, as of a lamb unblemished and spotless, *the blood* of Christ." 1 Peter 1:18-19

We were justified by His blood:

"Much more then, having now been justified by His blood, we shall be saved from the wrath *of God* through Him." Romans 5:9

We have forgiveness by His blood:

"And according to the Law, *one may* almost *say,* all things are cleansed with blood, and without shedding of blood there is no forgiveness." Hebrews 9:22

We have been sanctified by His blood:

"Therefore Jesus also, that He might sanctify the people through His own blood, suffered outside the gate." Hebrews 13:12

We have been reconciled to God by His blood:

"For if while we were enemies we were reconciled

to God through the death of His Son, much more, having been reconciled, we shall be saved by His life." Romans 5:10

"Therefore, we are ambassadors for He made Him who knew no sin *to be* sin on our behalf, so that we might become the righteousness of God in Him. Christ, as though God were making an appeal through us; we beg you on behalf of Christ, be reconciled to God." 2 Corinthians 5:20

We have been made righteous by His blood:
"But now apart from the Law *the* righteousness of God has been manifested, being witnessed by the Law and the Prophets, even *the* righteousness of God through faith in Jesus Christ for all those who believe; for there is no distinction;" Romans 3:21-22

We have been purified by His blood:
"And according to the Law, *one may* almost *say,* all things are *cleansed* with blood, and without shedding of blood there is no forgiveness." Hebrews 9:22

"Since you have in obedience to the truth purified your souls for a sincere love of the brethren, fervently love one another from the heart." 1 Peter 1:22

We have peace with God through His blood:
"Therefore, having been justified by faith, we have peace with God through our Lord Jesus Christ, through whom also we have obtained our introduction by faith into this grace in which we stand; and we exult in hope of the glory of God." Romans 5:1-2

We have power over the enemy through His blood:
"...and what is the surpassing greatness of His power toward us who believe. *These are* in accordance

with the working of the strength of His might which He brought about in Christ, when He raised Him from the dead and seated Him at His right hand in the heavenly *places,* far above all rule and authority and power and dominion, and every name that is named, not only in this age but also in the one to come." Ephesians 1:19-21

Through His blood we receive the Glory of God:

"… to whom God willed to make known what is the riches of the glory of this mystery among the Gentiles, which is Christ in you, the hope of glory." Colossians 1:27

We have protection through His blood:

"…who are protected by the power of God through faith for a salvation ready to be revealed in the last time." 1 Peter 1:5

We have healing through His blood:

"…and He Himself bore our sins in His body on the cross, so that we might die to sin and live to righteousness; for by His wounds you were healed." 1 Peter 2:24

We have victory over sin through His blood:

"For the death that He died, He died to sin once for all; but the life that He lives, He lives to God. Even so consider yourselves to be dead to sin, but alive to God in Christ Jesus." Romans 6:10-11

"And they overcame him because of the blood of the Lamb and because of the word of their testimony, and they did not love their life even when faced with death." Revelation 12:11

Deliverance is in the cross,
not in our fleshly activity.

THE CATALYST

Since 1975 all cars with internal combustion engines have used catalytic converters to reduce emissions. In chemistry, a catalyst is a substance that causes or accelerates a chemical reaction without itself being affected. Catalytic converters are designed to reduce three harmful emissions in automobiles; they are carbon monoxide, hydrocarbons and nitrogen oxides. To accomplish this the harmful gasses produced by the engine pass down the exhaust pipe, through the catalytic converter and out the tail pipe. The job of the catalytic converter is to convert harmful pollutants into less harmful emissions before they leave the car's exhaust system.

The catalytic converter contains ceramic beads or a honeycomb structure that is coated with something that is more precious than gold; it is coated with platinum; in fact, platinum is a by-product of a gold mine. Some of the newer vehicles use platinum, rhodium, palladium and even gold as a catalyst in the catalytic converter.

Many have seen or heard of photochemical smog. Photochemical smog is a condition that develops when primary pollutants such as oxides of nitrogen and volatile organic compounds, (VOC's) created from fossil fuels interact under the influence of sunlight. What happens is morning traffic increases the emissions of nitrogen oxides and VOC's as people drive to work. The nitrogen oxides and VOC's react forming nitrogen dioxide. As the sun becomes more intense, the nitrogen dioxide is broken down and its by-products form concentrations of ozone. As the sun goes down, the production of ozone is halted. Because they have a lot of sunlight Denver and L.A. have among the highest occurrences of photochemical smog. If I were a chemist I could explain all the chemical equations of how a catalyst works and I would probably bore you to death.

There is, however, another catalyst at work in the world today. It's not a chemical catalyst but a spiritual catalyst, and it too is more precious than gold. This catalyst is so precious that it cannot be purchased at any price; it can only be received by grace through faith. This catalyst is the precious blood of Jesus Christ that was poured out on the cross at Calvary. When it is applied it is capable of turning the blackest sin into something that is whiter than snow. The blood of Jesus Christ, God's son, cleanses us from all sin. 1 John 1:7. As platinum causes a chemical reaction to turn something harmful into something good, the blood of Jesus Christ causes a spiritual reaction, and those who are cleansed by it are changed from something harmful into something good.

There are certain laws that have been set into motion on this earth and cannot be changed; such as the law of gravity and the law of sowing and reaping. "Whatsoever a man sows that shall he also reap." Galatians 6:7. Another law that cannot be changed says: "The life of the flesh is in the blood and I have given it to you on the altar to make atonement for your souls; for it is the blood by reason of the life that makes atonement." Leviticus 17:11. Without the shedding of blood there is no remission of sin. Just as a catalytic converter changes things, so too a true conversion brought about by the blood of Jesus Christ changes things. You are converted from a sinner to saint in a moment of time.

As sunlight causes photochemical smog as it reacts with the nitrogen oxides, the Son light exposes the darkness of our hearts that can only be changed by the blood of Jesus. If I were a theologian I could probably explain how all this works, but for now I just know that it does.

THE TESTIMONY THAT OVERCOMES

"Now the salvation, and the power, and the kingdom of our God and the authority of His Christ have come, for the accuser of our brethren has been thrown down, who accuses them before our God day and night. And they overcame him because of the blood of the Lamb and because of the word of their testimony, and they did not love their life even when faced with death." Revelation 12:10-11

The testimony that overcomes the enemy is the testimony that declares what we have, and who we are in Christ, as we look at the finished work of Christ. In Christendom we are accustomed to people giving their testimony of how they once were lost, but now they're saved. That is a good confession, and it has its place, but it's not necessarily the kind of testimony that overcomes the enemy. Often times it is nothing more than giving attention to the enemies' works that he does not deserve. Sometimes the only thing better than the sinning is the telling. The enemy is like a spoiled child; he just wants attention and he doesn't care what kind of attention it is, good or bad; he doesn't care as long as he gets attention. We don't need to get into a contest to see who has the worst testimony; that is not the kind of testimony that overcomes the enemy.

In Christ, I am Redeemed — A price had to be paid and He paid it. He paid a debt that He did not owe because we owed a debt that we could not pay. I was saved, I am being saved, and one of these days I will be saved. I have quit worrying about my salvation; it is a done deal. "Knowing that you were not redeemed with perishable things like silver or gold from your futile way of life inherited from your forefathers, but with precious blood, as of a lamb unblemished and spotless, the blood of Christ." 1 Peter 1:18-19

In Christ, I am Justified — Just as if I had never sinned. "Therefore, having been justified by faith, we have peace with God through our Lord Jesus Christ." Romans 5:1 I now have peace with God. I don't have to try to have peace with God.

In Christ, I am Sanctified — Regeneration. "...but you were washed, but you were sanctified, but you were justified in the name of the Lord Jesus Christ, and in the Spirit of our God." 1 Corinthians 6:11 It is not me struggling to live the Christian life. He never asked me to. He asked me to allow Him to live His life through me. It is surrender, as I allow Him to live His life through me. Not my *trying* but *trusting*.

In Christ, I am Delivered — "For He delivered us from the domain of darkness, and transferred us to the kingdom of His beloved Son." Colossians 1:13

In Christ, I am Protected — "...who are *protected by the power of God* through faith for a salvation ready to be revealed in the last time." 1 Peter 1:5 In Christ I am safe. I do not have to worry about myself. I am protected by the power of God. This boat can't sink with Jesus on board. Fear has no part in me. If I am not safe in the lion's den with Jesus, then I'm not safe anywhere.

In Christ, I am Dead to Sin — "...knowing this, that our old self was crucified with Him, that our body of sin might be done away with, that we should no longer be slaves to sin." Romans 6:6

In Christ, I am dead to the Law — "There is therefore now no condemnation for those who are in Christ Jesus." Romans 8: 1 "Therefore my brethren, you also were made to die to the Law through the body of Christ, that you might be joined to another, to Him who was raised from the dead, that we might bear fruit for God." Romans 7:4 'But now we have been released from the Law, having died to that by which we were bound, so that we serve in newness of the Spirit and not in oldness of the letter." Romans 7:6

In Christ, I am Alive to God — "Even so consider yourselves to be dead to sin, but alive to God in Christ Jesus." Romans 6:11

In Christ, I am Righteous — "But to the one who does not work, but believes in Him who justifies the ungodly, his faith is reckoned as righteousness." Romans 4:5 "...and may be found in Him, not having a righteousness of my own derived from the law, but that which is through faith in Christ, the righteousness which comes from God on the basis of faith." Philippians 3:9

In Christ, I am Forgiven — Colossians 2:13 "...He made us alive together with Him, having forgiven us all our transgressions."

In Christ, I have Eternal Life — "That whoever believes will in Him have eternal life. For God so loved the world, that He gave His only begotten Son, that whoever believes in Him shall not perish, but have eternal life." John 3:15-16

In Christ, I am Healed — "He himself bore our sins in

His body on the cross, that we might die to sin and live to righteousness, for by His wounds you were healed." 1 Peter 2:24

This is just a partial list of who we are in Christ Jesus. We haven't even touched upon the fruit or the gifts of the Spirit. As good as it is, the Christian life is so much more than, simply going to heaven when you die. It is living here on earth in the power of His resurrection, daily allowing Him to live His life in you.

What do you think would happen if you were to pretend that God's word was true? Do you think it would have a tendency to change your life?

Let's pretend that God's word is true.

Let's pretend that Jesus Christ is alive.

Let's pretend that God is living in you.

Let's pretend that God will protect you wherever He leads you.

Let's pretend that no weapon formed against you shall prosper.

Let's pretend that God will supply all your needs.

Let's pretend that God will guide your every step.

Now I dare you to believe these things for they are true.

"What shall I render to the Lord for all His benefits toward me? I shall lift up the cup of salvation, and call upon the name of the Lord." Psalm 116:12-13

Now, go live your testimony.

The Glory of Man
Section Three

Identity

IDENTITY

In these days of uncertainty many have lost their way and do not know who they are, or where they are going. We hear of many going through an "identity crisis." Many are identified by their work, and if they lose their job or retire, they have lost their identity. Others may have their identity in what they own. They take great pride in things. If these things are lost or taken away in a financial crisis or divorce, they have lost their identity and are devastated. You hear of teenagers trying to figure out who they are, and many times they look in all the wrong places as they seek their identity. We hear about identity thieves who steal your personal identification and seek to destroy you financially.

All people have a physical identity whether good or bad, and I can identify you by the deeds of your flesh, (human nature) that are dominant in your life. I can say, "Oh! Look here comes Joe, the dominant bully." or, "Here comes Sally, the shy, timid one." Or, "Tom, the arrogant one." We are physically identified by the traits we exude. These traits come from the heart of a person. "For out of the heart come evil thoughts, murders, adulteries, fornications, thefts, false witness and slanders." Matthew 15:19. The Bible further describes these things as the deeds of the flesh, (human nature) "…which are: immorality, impurity, sensuality, idolatry, sorcery, enmities, strife, jealousy, outbursts of anger, disputes, dissentions, factions, envying, drunkenness, carousing and things like these. And those who practice such things shall not inherit the Kingdom of God." Galatians 5:19-21

But, more importantly all people also have a spiritual identity. As we grow in Christ our spiritual identity begins to overshadow our physical identity as our physical identity begins to become less dominant. "He must increase, but I must decrease." John 3:30 "We are being changed from glory to glory." 2 Corinthians 3:18 It has been said I have two lions in me; a good lion and a bad lion. The one that is the strongest is the one I feed the most. As certain things are true in the physical realm so also are they true in the spiritual realm. Once you have given your life to Christ you can no longer use your human nature as an excuse for your sin. Your identity can no longer be your alibi. You have heard people say: "I was born this way." We were all born with a bent towards certain sins. You've heard it said: "That guy is a born liar." That may very well be true. He may have been born with a bent or a tendency to lie. That doesn't make it right or excuse what he does, neither does it mean that the Lord can't change that person into His image.

We are changed into His image by the infilling of the Spirit of God as His Spirit indwells our spirit. As you know, an apple tree does not need to struggle to produce apples. The apples come as a natural consequence of being a healthy apple tree. "The fruit of the Spirit is love, joy, peace, patience, kindness, goodness, faithfulness, gentleness, self-control." Galatians 5:22-23 "The fruit of the light consists in all goodness and righteousness and truth." Ephesians 5:9 These things are the natural effects of the Spirit of God living in us. As an apple tree does not need to struggle to produce apples, we don't need to struggle to produce His fruit in us. We need to remember that it is His fruit, not ours. We can hinder the working of God in our lives, but we can't help Him. It's got to be His work as He produces His fruit in us. That way all the glory goes to Him. The best thing we can do is to let Him.

IDENTIFICATION — BAPTISM

The Main Principle
The main principle is found in Romans chapter 7:1-4

"Or do you not know, brethren (for I am speaking to those who know the law), that the law has jurisdiction over a person as long as he lives?

For the married woman is bound by law to her husband while he is living, but if her husband dies, she is released from the law concerning the husband.

So then if, while her husband is living, she is joined to another man, she shall be called an adulteress, but if her husband dies, she is free from the law, so that she is not an adulteress, though she is joined to another man.

Therefore, my brethren, you also were made to die to the Law through the body of Christ, that you might be joined to another, to Him who was raised from the dead, that we might bear fruit for God."

The above passage is not a teaching about marriage, it is giving the basic principle about our relationship to the Law. The same principle holds true for our dealing with sin, the flesh and the world. Our victory is found in the death, burial and resurrection of Jesus Christ. Although this happened over two thousand years ago it does not become effective in our daily experience until we reckon, (or count it as true) in our daily walk.

We somehow believe: "Now that He died for my sins, in my stead, the least that I could do to show my appreciation is to try hard to live the Christian life." Not true, the answer to our problem can only be found in Christ, not in our trying.

Nowhere does the Bible say that we should try hard to live the Christian Life. The only one capable of living the Christian life is Jesus Christ Himself. It does say, however, that we need to allow Him to live His life in and through us.

We won't need victory over sin when we die and go to heaven. There will be no presence of sin in heaven to have victory over. We need victory over sin here, now, on our way to heaven. We won't need healing when we get to heaven. There will be no presence of sickness in heaven. We need healing, now, on our way to heaven.

"Any teaching which detracts from the centrality of Christ under the pretense of leading men to maturity and perfection is a perversion that threatens the very essence of the faith." [1]

According to Wycliffe: "The book of Colossians makes anathema any belief or practice that displaces the centrality of Jesus as redeemer and the perfecter of His people."

2 Corinthians 10:5 "We are destroying speculations and every lofty thing raised up against the knowledge of God. And we are taking every thought captive to the obedience of Christ."

"If any man is in Christ he is a new creature; old things passed away; behold new things have come." Corinthians 5:17

From the Writings of Watchman Nee

"If the effect of the Cross were limited to the substitutional side — that is to say, the side that causes people not to perish but have eternal life — the salvation God gives would still be incomplete. Though this would save people from the penalty of sin, it would not save them from the power sin has over their lives. For this reason, the Savior completed a twofold work: He saved people from the penalty of sin, and He saved them from the power and control sin has over them. Sadly, many only take advantage of the former!"

"God's Word does not say that the old man needs to be washed. This old man — the sin factor — is corrupted beyond repair. Therefore, God's way of dealing with the old man is to put it to death. This is accomplished through a union of the old man with the Lord Jesus in crucifixion. An ignorance of this fact explains why so many live in defeat. Apart from dying with Christ, there is no other way to put the old man to death, (Galatians. 2:20) and apart from putting the old man to death, there is no way to live in victory."

"What is the consequence of having this sin factor — the old man — crucified? The *body of Sin* is *done away with*. (Romans 6:6) Done away with means *rendered powerless*."

"The way you obtain the substitutionary death of the Lord Jesus is the way you enter into co-death with Him — by believing! All who believe in the substitutionary death of Christ are saved; all who believe in the co-death with Christ overcome sin."

"The old man is not crucified by touch or feel; he is crucified by reckoning, (Romans 6:11). Whenever a believer fails to reckon, his old man is revived; but if he truly reckons, there will be supernatural power coming to him."

"When the Lord Jesus was on the cross, He had authority to come down if He so wished. By the same token, those who are crucified with the Lord can let their old man come down from the cross, if they so choose." [2]

We have three enemies; the devil, the world and our flesh. When battling our enemy, the devil, you cast him out in the power of Jesus Christ, stand firm, or flee. When battling the world, our flesh or sin we are to look at the finished work of Christ and reckon ourselves having died to those things with Him on the cross.

"For you have died and your life is hidden with Christ in God." Colossians 3:3

"Knowing this, that our old self was crucified with Him, that our body of sin might be done away with, that we should no longer be slaves to sin." Romans 6:6

"Now those who belong to Christ Jesus have crucified the flesh with its passions and desires." Galatians 5:24

"But may it never be that I would boast, except, in the cross of the Lord Jesus Christ, through which the world has been crucified to me, and I to the world." Galatians 6:14

• • •

Suppose you have a person in Kansas who wants to know what Pikes Peak's like. You travel up Pikes Peak and bring him a granite boulder, you tell him it is a big mountain composed of this type of rock. The boulder may have come from Pikes Peak and it was part of Pikes Peak, but it does a very poor job of describing what the Peak is like.

The same thing happens when we attempt to tell people the gospel of the Lord Jesus Christ. We bring to them a small boulder and present it to them in such a way that they believe that it is the whole. We present to them how Jesus paid the price for our sin, and if they believe and accept that they have heard the whole truth of the gospel and they will go to heaven when they die.

Many churches present only the substitutional side of the cross, and they can do that year after year, sermon after sermon in a hundred different ways and believe that they have done their job and have presented the gospel. They have only taken one boulder and presented it as the whole. Though this would save people from the penalty of their sin, it would not save them from the power sin has over their lives. For this reason, the savior presented a twofold work. He saved people from the penalty of their sin, and He saved them from the power and control sin has over them. Sadly, many only take advantage of the former! He saved us from the penalty of our sin and the power of sin and one day He will save us from the presence of sin. We won't need victory over the power of sin when we die and go to heaven; there won't be any sin. We need the victory over the power of sin in our lives now as we are on our way to heaven.

We are to receive victory over sin in our lives the same way as we received salvation by grace through faith. "As ye have received Christ Jesus the Lord so walk ye in Him." Scripture tells us that we are dead to the law, the flesh, sin and the world. I've heard it preached that these things are our *positional* standing in Christ not *actual*. My answer to that is, "Soldiers! Take Your Position." How can we deny what Jesus has done and claim that we have presented the gospel? That is the gospel! Paul tells us that we are to reckon on these things. Reckon means to count it as true. As we appropriate the finished work of Christ in our lives, or count it as true, we begin to walk in Christ. His death was over two thousand years ago, and we died with Him two thousand years ago; it only becomes real to us today as we reckon it so in our daily experience.

I have heard pastors tell people they need to try harder to overcome sin in their lives. I have read through the Bible numerous times and I've never seen the passage where it tells us we need to try harder. I have seen, however, where we are told to appropriate the death, burial and resurrection of Jesus Christ. I know of people, right now in our church, who are using worldly ways to overcome alcohol addictions and pornography. There are probably more that I don't know about. There are others who are involved in yoga, Hinduism and all kinds of metaphysical entrapments because we have not preached the gospel. This is an indictment against our churches.

Seems like the only answer many churches have is no better than what the world has to offer. The churches are relying on programs and other worldly methods. What should set the church apart is the blood of Jesus Christ, otherwise we are simply a nice club like the Rotary and Kiwanis clubs. If we are going to deny and ignore the power of the blood of Jesus Christ, then you join your club and I'll join mine. The church should be changing the world, not the world changing the church.

• • •

We have all heard about the substitutionary death of Christ, but we have heard little about the daily victory we have in Christ through our identification with Him in His death, burial and resurrection. This has been provided for us through the fact that we have died with Him to the law, our flesh, sin and the world. Either one of two things are true: (1) We do not know these truths or, (2) We have willfully chosen to ignore them. If there is ignorance of these truths that are taught in Romans 6, Galatians 3 and all of the Epistles that is one thing.

But if we know these truths and have chosen to ignore them, that is quite another thing.

The following quotations are what many great gospel teachers have taught through the years. Perhaps it would be wise to listen to them: The following quotes are from *Principles of Spiritual Growth,* also known as the *Green letters,* Miles Stanford. Published by Back to the Bible.

> Evan H. Hopkins: "The trouble of the believer who knows Christ as his justification is not sin as to its guilt, but sin as to its ruling power. In other words, it is not from sin as a load, or an offence, that he seeks to be freed—for he sees that God has completely acquitted him from the charge and penalty of sin—but it is from sin as a master. To know God's way of deliverance from sin as a master he must apprehend the truth contained in the sixth chapter of Romans. There we see what God has done, not with our sins—that question the Apostle dealt with in the preceding chapters—but with ourselves, the agents and slaves of sin. He has put our old man—our original self—where He put our sins, namely, on the cross with Christ. 'Knowing this, that our old man was crucified with him,' (Romans 6:6). The believer there sees not only that Christ died for him—substitution—but that he died with Christ—identification." *Thoughts on Life and Godliness, p. 50*

> Andrew Murray: "Like Christ, the believer too has died to sin; he is one with Christ, in the likeness of His death (Romans 6:5). And as the knowledge that Christ died for sin as our atonement is indispensable to our justification; so the knowledge that Christ and we with Him in the likeness of His death, are dead to sin, is indispensable to our sanctification." *Like Christ, p. 176*

J. Hudson Taylor: "Since Christ has thus dwelt in my heart by faith, how happy I have been! I am dead and buried with Christ—ay, and risen too! And now Christ lives in me, and 'the life which I now live in the flesh I live by the faith of the Son of God, who loved me, and gave himself for me' [Gal. 2:20]. Nor should we look upon this experience, these truths, as for the few. They are the birthright of every child of God, and no one can dispense with them without dishonoring our Lord." *Spiritual Secret, p.* 116

William R. Newell: "To those who refuse or neglect to reckon themselves dead to sin as God commands, we press the question, 'How are you able to believe that Christ really bare the guilt of your sins and that you will not meet them at the judgment day?' It is only *God's Word* that tells you Christ bare your sins in His own body on the tree. And it is *that same Word* that tells you that you, as connected with Adam, died with Christ, that your old man was crucified, that since you are in Christ you shared His death unto sin, and are thus to reckon your present relation to sin in Christ— as one who is dead to it, and alive unto God." *Romans, Verse by Verse, p.* 227

Lewis Sperry Chafer: "The theme under consideration is concerned with the death of Christ as that death is related to the divine judgments of the sin nature in the child of God. The necessity for such judgments and the sublime revelation that these judgments are now fully accomplished for us is unfolded in Romans 6:1-10. This passage is the foundation as well as the key to the possibility of a 'walk in the Spirit'." *He That Is Spiritual, p.* 154

Ruth Paxson: "The old 'I' in you and me was judicially crucified with Christ. 'Ye died' and your death dates from the death of Christ. The old man, the old Self in God's reckoning was taken to the Cross with Christ and crucified and taken into the tomb with Christ and buried. Assurance of deliverance from the sphere of the 'flesh' and of the dethronement of 'the old man' rests upon the apprehension and acceptance of this fact of co-crucifixion." *Life on the Highest Plane,* Vol. II, pp. 78, 79

Watchman Nee: "The Blood can wash away my sins, but it cannot wash away my 'old man.' It needs the cross to crucify me the sinner. Our sins are dealt with by the Blood, but we ourselves are dealt with by the Cross. The Blood procures our pardon; the Cross procures our deliverance from what we are." *The Normal Christian Life,* pp. 31, 32

L.E. Maxwell: "Believers in Christ were joined to Him at the cross, united to Him in death and resurrection. We died with Christ. He died for us, and we died with Him. This is a great fact, true of all believers." *Christian Victory, p.* 11

Norman B. Harrison: "This is the distinctive mark of the Christian—the experience of the cross. Not merely that Christ died for us, but that we died with Him. 'Knowing this, that our old man is crucified with him'. (Romans 6:6)" *His Side Versus Our Side, p.* 40

F.J. Huegel: "If the great Luther, with his stirring message of justification by faith, had with Paul moved on from Romans 5 to Romans 6 with its amazing declarations concerning the now justified sinner's position of identification with his crucified Lord, would not a stifled Protestantism be on higher ground today? Might it not be free from its ulcerous fleshiness?" *The Cross of Christ, p.* 84

Alexander R. Hay: "The believer has been united with Christ in His death. In this union with Christ, the flesh, 'the body of sin'—the entire fallen, sin-ruined being with its intelligence, will and desires—is judged and crucified. By faith, the believer reckons (counts) himself 'dead unto sin.' (Romans 6:3-14)" 1V.T. *Order for Church & Missionary*, p. 310

T. Austin-Sparks: "The first phase of our spiritual experience may be a great and overflowing joy, with a marvelous sense of emancipation. In this phase extravagant things are often said as to total deliverance and final victory. Then there may, and often does, come a phase of which inward conflict is the chief feature. It may be very much of a Romans seven experience. This will lead, under the Lord's hand, to the fuller knowledge of the meaning of identification with Christ, as in Romans six. Happy the man who has been instructed in this from the beginning." *What Is Man? p.* 61

J. Penn-Lewis: "If the difference between 'Christ dying for us,' and 'our dying with Him,' has not been recognized, acknowledged, and applied, it may safely be affirmed that the self is still the dominating factor in the life." *Memoir, p.* 26

William Culbertson: "Who died on the cross? Of course, our blessed Lord died on the cross; but who else died there? 'Knowing this, that our old man was crucified with him, that the body of sin might be done away, that we should no longer be in bondage to sin; for he that hath died is justified from sin. But if we died with Christ, we believe that we shall also live with him.' (Rom. 6:6-8)" *God's Provision for Holy Living, p.* 46

Reginald Wallis: "God says in effect, 'My child, as you reckoned on the substitutionary work of the Lord Jesus Christ for your salvation, now go a step farther and reckon on His representative work for your victory day by day.' You believe the Lord Jesus died for your sins because God said so. Now take the next step. Accept by faith the further fact that you died with Him, i.e., that your 'old man was crucified with Him'." *The New Life, p. 51*

James R. McConkey: "Because He died 'death hath no more dominion over Him,' and because of our union with Him 'sin shall not have dominion over you,' even though it is present in you. Our 'reckoning' ourselves dead to sin in Jesus Christ does not make it a fact—it is already a fact through our union with Him. Our reckoning it to be true only makes us begin to realize the fact in experience." *The Way of Victory*

I pray that Christians would appropriate the finished work of Christ and therein find the victory they have been seeking.

BAPTISM OUR IDENTIFICATION
Glory Restored
The baptism of the Holy Spirit is the ongoing work of the Holy Spirit to identify us with the finished work of the Lord Jesus Christ.

The word *baptism* has two meanings: the literal word and the metaphorical word. The literal meaning of the word baptize means to plunge, to dip, to immerse. The word baptize, metaphorically means a change of identity, to identify, identification. The metaphorical meaning has little to do with water. You may better associate it with the words, *united with*, or *put into*, instead of identified with.

When speaking of the baptism of the Holy Spirit it is important to understand the word baptism in the metaphorical sense. By using the word *identify*, or *identification*, we can understand the work and purpose of the Holy Spirit. "He shall glorify Me; for He shall take of Mine, and shall disclose it to you." John 16:14 And again in John 15:26-27 "When the helper comes, whom I will send from the Father, that is the Spirit of Truth, who proceeds from the Father, *He will bear witness of Me, and you will bear witness also.*"

To transliterate is to spell in the characters of another alphabet; it does not give the meaning of the word. A true translation gives the meaning of the word. The Greek word baptize was transliterated and therefore its meaning must be interpreted in the light of its context. If the Greek word *baptizo* had been translated rather than transliterated, then we would have read "Go ye therefore, and teach all nations, *identifying them* in the Name of the Father, and the Son, and of the Holy Spirit." Matthew 28:19

Or again we would better understand words of the forerunner, John the Identifier: "I indeed baptize (identify) you with water; but one mightier than I cometh, the latchet of whose shoes I am not worthy to unloose; He shall baptize (identify) you with the Holy Spirit and fire." Luke 3:16 Again in Mark 16:16 "He who has believed and has been baptized (identified with Christ) shall be saved; but he who has disbelieved shall be condemned." Mark 1:8 "I baptize you with water; but He will baptize (identify) you with the Holy Spirit."

The baptism (identification) of the Holy Spirit is the ongoing work of the Holy Spirit to identify us with the finished work of the Lord Jesus Christ. Some things He did as our *example*; Such as when He knew He had an important meeting the next day to choose the twelve apostles. He spent all night in prayer seeking God's will and having fellowship with the Father. Luke 6: 12. "And it was at this time He went off to the mountain to pray, and He spent the whole night in prayer to God." Other things He did as our *substitute* such as His death on the cross as payment for our sins. We must understand and appropriate what He did for us on our journey back to glory.

• • •

To prepare for Passover an Israelite would choose a lamb from his sheep-fold that was without spot or blemish. This he would do on the tenth day of the month of Nisan. He would take it into the house and keep it for three days. Then he examined it again, and on the next day, the fourteenth day of Nisan, he killed it. The killing of this lamb looked forward to the day when God would send His lamb to be the final and complete sacrifice for sin.

There came a day when John the Baptist saw Jesus coming toward him at the Jordan River and said "Behold, the Lamb of God, who takes away the sin of the world." John 1:29 John, the identifier, points to Jesus as the Passover Lamb. After His baptism a voice was heard from heaven, saying, "This is my beloved Son; in whom I am well pleased." Luke 3:22 and Mark 1:11 NKJV. He was not only identified by John, but also identified by the Father. After three years He was again identified by the Father on the Mount of Transfiguration. Once more the majestic voice was heard from heaven. "This is my beloved Son, in whom I am well pleased; hear ye Him." Matthew 17:5 KJV The identification was now complete. Then the Lamb was taken out of the house, he was taken outside the gate, and gave His life for our sins. "Therefore Jesus also, that He might sanctify the people through His own blood, suffered outside the gate." Hebrews 13:12

• • •

The baptism of the Holy Spirit, or identification, is the ongoing work of the Holy Spirit in the life of a Christian. The result is not only a *changed life*, but also an *exchanged life*.

We are identified with Christ in His conception, birth, circumcision, ministry, baptism, life, death, burial and resurrection. Not only are we identified with Christ in His physical body, but also into His spiritual body, the church. It is the Holy Spirit's job to take the things of Christ and show them unto us. John 15:26

Heavenly Father; Your Holy Bible is truth. It's light, alive, and powerful. It's pure, and is absolutely sufficient. It is our lifeline! How would any of us, in the modern era, ever have come to faith...come to know You without it? Thank You fervently, that through Your book, You told us as sinners, of our lost spiritual condition, it's consequences, and Your provision. Furthermore; within it's pages, You unerringly teach Your children how to live the Christian life and how to ask for and receive Your gracious enablement's. This magnificent revelation of Your nature and character...of Your ways and plans for mankind, proclaims majestic doctrinal truths for the entire body of believers. Thank You for them... for the flawless record of our Redeemer's death...His burial...His resurrection...and of His ascension, His glorification, and His soon coming. Thank You that You not only allowed Him to die on our behalf, but also put us to death, buried, resurrected, ascended, seated and glorified us together with and in Him. (Prayer by John Hayes)

In order to firmly establish the identity principal, we will begin our trek on our path to glory by looking at the law and our relationship to it.

THE LAW AND US
The Purpose of the Law

The Law is perfect and just and good. He did not give it that man might be saved by it, but to prove to men that they were sinners.

"Now we know that whatever the Law says, it speaks to those who are under the Law, that every mouth may be closed, and all the world may become accountable to God; because by the works of the Law no flesh will be justified in his sight; for through the Law comes the knowledge of sin." Romans 3:19-20

"So then, the Law is holy, and the commandment is holy and righteous and good." Romans 7:12

"Why the Law then? It was added because of transgressions, <u>until</u> the seed should come to whom the promise had been made." (Christ) Galatians 3:19

The law makes me see that I am a sinner and constantly condemns me. We know that it is right and holy and just, and we know that no matter how hard we try, we just can't be good enough. We just can't live up to its standards under our own power. It does not give me the power to live a godly life. It has no power to keep me from sinning. The Israelites tried it for 1500 years and failed. If it were possible for one person to keep the law, Christ would not have had to die. That one person would have proved that it was possible. If you think the law is hard to keep, try the Sermon on the Mount. Matthew 5

"For I say to you, that unless your righteousness surpasses that of the scribes and Pharisees, you shall not enter, the kingdom of heaven." Matthew 5:20

"If a law had been given which was able to impart life, then righteousness would indeed have been based on law." Galatians 3:21

What God Did

"What the Law could not do, God did." Romans 8:3

"Do not think that I came to abolish the Law or the Prophets; I did not come to abolish, but to fulfill." Matthew 5:17

Romans chapter 7 tells us what God did to free us from the constant condemnation of the Law of Sin and Death, so that we could be joined to the Spirit of Life in Christ Jesus.

We were married to the Law, and we were bound by the marriage commitment until the death of one of the partners. The Law could not die because it was ordained by God.

> "Therefore, my brethren, you also were made to die to the Law through the body of Christ, that you might be joined to another, to Him who was raised from the dead, that we might bear fruit for God." Romans 7:4

> "But now we have been released from the Law, having died to that by which we were bound, so that we serve in newness of the Spirit and not in oldness of the letter." Romans 7:6

We are now under Grace not under the law. The law can no longer condemn us, we are free from its curse. God freed us from the law so that we might be joined to Christ. God freed us from the law so that He might live out His righteousness in us Himself.

Married to the Law	Married to Christ
(Sin & Death)	(Spirit of Life)
Died To	Alive To
DO	DONE
Try	Trust
Flesh	Faith
Sinai	Calvary
Condemn	Convict

We cannot earn or work for God's blessings. We already have them.

> "You foolish Galatians, ...did you receive the Spirit by the works of the Law, or by hearing with faith? Are

you so foolish? Having begun by the Spirit, are you now being perfected by the flesh? Does He then, who provides you with the Spirit and works miracles among you, do it by the works of the Law, or by hearing with faith?" Galatians 3:1-5

"Christ redeemed us from the curse of the Law, having become a curse for us — for it is written, 'Cursed is everyone who hangs on a tree' — in order that in Christ Jesus the blessing of Abraham might come to the Gentiles, so that we might receive the promise of the Spirit through faith." Galatians 3:13-14

The Galatians were spiritual adulterers. Married to one (Christ) trying to have an affair with another (Law). "You have been severed from Christ, you who are seeking to be justified by law: you have fallen from grace." Galatians 5:4 "As you therefore have received Christ Jesus the Lord, so walk in Him." Colossians 2:6

"And six days later Jesus took with Him Peter and James and John his brother, and brought them up to a high mountain by themselves. And he was transfigured before them; and His face shone like the sun, and His garments became as white as light. And behold, Moses (Law) and Elijah (Prophets) appeared to them, talking with him. And Peter answered and said to Jesus, 'Lord, it is good for us to be here; if You wish, I will make three tabernacles here, one for You, and one for Moses (Law), and one for Elijah (Prophets).' While he was still speaking, behold, a bright cloud overshadowed them; and behold, a voice out of the cloud, saying. 'This is My beloved Son, with whom I am well-pleased; hear Him!' And when the disciples heard this, they fell on their faces and were much afraid. And Jesus came to them and touched them and said, 'Arise, and do not be afraid.' And lifting up their eyes, they saw no one, except Jesus Himself alone." Matthew 17:1-8

We do not need three tabernacles, (1) the law, (2) the prophets, (3) and Jesus. We just need Jesus.

"Do not think I came to abolish the Law or the Prophets; I did not come to abolish, but to fulfill." Matthew 5:17

"You shall love the Lord your God with all your heart, and with all your soul and with all your mind. This is the great and foremost commandment. And a second is like it, You shall love your neighbor as yourself. On these two commandments depend the whole Law and the Prophets." Matthew 22:37-40

He is for us...God! ...He suffered for us ...He died for us, He was buried for us...He rose for us...and He is coming back for us...He is our fortress...His name itself is a strong tower...the righteous run into it and are safe! He is our shield and buckler...He is our defense and He is our defender...He is the Captain of our salvation...He is for us! If God be for us who can be against us? He is for us! Thank you, Father, that He is for us. (Prayer by John Hayes)

IDENTIFIED IN HIS CONCEPTION

He Was Conceived as Man by The Holy Spirit
"And the angel answered and said to her, "the Holy Spirit will come upon you, and the power of the Most High will overshadow you; and for that reason the holy offspring shall be called the Son of God." Luke 1:35

"And Mary said, "Behold the bond-slave of the Lord; be it done to me according to your word," Luke 1:38

The very moment Mary spoke those words she conceived. She conceived the Word by the word of God.

> "Blessed is she who believed that there would be a fulfillment of what had been spoken to her by the Lord." Luke 1:45

We Are Conceived by The Holy Spirit on Our Path to Glory Restored

> "In the exercise of His will He brought us forth by the word of truth, so that we might be, as it were, the first fruits among His creatures." James 1:18

There came a time when the Holy Spirit came to you and revealed the Lord Jesus Christ to you. The moment you said; "Let it be done to me according to your word." You were conceived of the Holy Spirit, given life and He began the work of producing the Lord Jesus Christ in you. You conceived the Word by the word of God. Blessed are you who believed that there would be a fulfillment of what had been spoken to you by the Lord.

IDENTIFIED IN HIS BIRTH

Jesus, the Son of God, was born as the Son of Man, so that we who were born as the sons of man could become the sons of God. (To clarify the meaning of the word *son*, it helps to think *of the order of Jesus*, who was of the *order of God*, was born of the *order of man*, so that we who were born of the order of man could become born again of the order of God).

He Was Identified as Man at His Birth

In His birth he was identified to the shepherds by the angels of God. Luke 2:8-12

He was identified to the Magi by means of a star. Matthew 2:1-2

He was identified by Simeon in the temple. Luke 2:25-32

We Are Born of The Holy Spirit on Our Journey to Glory Restored

"Truly, truly, I say to you, unless one is born again, he cannot see the kingdom of God." John 3:3

"But as many as received Him, to them He gave the right to become children of God, even to those who believe in His Name, who were born not of blood, nor of the will of the flesh, nor of the will of man, but of God." John 1:12-13

"For you have been born again not of seed which is perishable but imperishable, that is, through the living and abiding word of God." 1 Peter 1:23

"In the exercise of His will He brought us forth by the word of truth, so that we might be, as it were, the first fruits among His creatures." James 1:18

Perhaps this is a good time to talk about adoption. You cannot be adopted into the family of God, you can only become a child of God by being born into the family.

ADOPTION

"The word *adoption* is used only by Paul, five times in the New Testament. He uses the Greek word *huiothesia*. These are found in Romans 8:15, 23; 9:4; Galatians 4:5, and Ephesians 1:5 When broken down, the word means *huios* — an adult son, *thesia* — placement. Paul is referring to a Greek and Roman custom rather than a Hebrew one. Since h*uiothesia* was a technical term in Roman law for an act that specific legal and social effects, there is much probability that Paul had some reference to that in his use of the word. Adoption, when thus legally performed, put a man in every respect in the position of a son by birth to him who had adopted him, so that he possessed the same rights and owed the same obligations. Being a *huios*, a son, involves the conformity of the child that has the life of God in him to the image, purposes, and interests of God and that spiritual family into which he is born. In eternity there will be a revelation by God which will indicate the measure of this conformity to God. Romans 8:19" [3]

> "For ye have not received the spirit of bondage again to fear; but ye have received the Spirit of adoption, whereby we cry, Abba, Father." Romans 8:15

You cannot be adopted into the family of God. The only way you can become a child of God is to be born into the family. "In Paul's epistles he uses the word adoption in a different way than we use the word adoption. This does not mean that all who preceded Christ were slaves or children and not sons. He is not comparing individuals with individuals, but rather a method of administration with another method of administration. The administration of the law from Moses to Christ brought with it fear. The administration of grace has made full provision for setting the child free from all fears and giving him a magnificent standing as a responsible son." [4]

There was a Roman and Greek ceremony that Paul was referring to. This ceremony was shown in the movie, *The Robe*. When a son had reached a certain age set forth by the father, he was taken to the temple where all the rights of the father were bestowed on the son. With speeches and much pomp, clean-shaven for the first time, he was given a family robe, a signet ring and sandals for his feet. From that time on he was never again treated as a child, but as a son with all the rights and privileges of the father.

Paul further explains this custom in Galatians 4:1-7.

> "Now I say, as long as the heir is a child, he does not differ at all from a slave although he is owner of everything, but he is under guardians and managers until the date set by the father. So also we, while we were children, were held in bondage under the elemental things of the world. But when the fullness

of the time came, God sent forth His Son, born of a woman, born under the Law, in order that He might redeem those who were under the law, that we might receive the adoption as sons. And because you are sons, God has sent forth the Spirit of His Son into our hearts, crying, "Abba! Father!" Therefore you are no longer a slave, but a son; and if a son, then an heir through God."

This act in the Roman and Greek culture was called *adoption.* This can be compared to *Bar Mitzvah* in the Hebrew culture, *age of accountability* in the evangelical culture, or *confirmation* in the Catholic and high church culture.

We have been adopted into an official position in the family of God. The difference between a child and a son is one of our *position*, not our *ownership*. We may turn to our heavenly Father with utter calmness and with full confidence that He cannot turn us away. Because of our position as sons, we have the right to use His name, speak in His name and pray in His name. This is involved in our position; this is guaranteed in our sonship.

Notice in the story of the prodigal son as recorded in Luke 15:11-32. When the son returned in verse 22, the father said to his slaves, "Quickly bring out the best robe and put it on him, and put a ring on his hand and sandals on his feet," All the rights and privileges as a son were instantly bestowed on him again. The real prodigal was the older son who, although he had all the rights and privileges of a son bestowed on him, refused to take his position as a son and continued to act as a child or slave.

There are those who refuse to come to the Lord for healing or restoration due to some past sin. They feel that they must suffer the consequences of their actions and therefore the Lord will not heal them. Tell me how much suffering is enough? You may have been carrying that burden for many years. It has kept you from walking in all the rights and privileges that are yours in Christ Jesus. When we allow the sins of our past to destroy our future it's as though the locust has come in and destroyed your crops. Me must put these things under the blood of Jesus Christ and remember, "The Blood of Jesus Christ God's Son cleanses us from all sin." 1 John 1:7 Our sins of the past, the present, and the future have all been cleansed by the blood.

> "Then I will make up to you for the years that the swarming locust has eaten." Joel 2:25

> "He predestined us to adoption as sons through Jesus Christ to Himself, according to the kind intention of His will." Ephesians 1:5

Every born-again child of God is predestined to be placed as a son with all the rights and privileges of the Father. We are not to stay as a child —but take our position as a son. One of these days we will see the complete culmination of these rights, but until then we need to stand in our position as given to us by the Lord Jesus Christ.

> "...but also we ourselves, having the first fruits of the Spirit, even we ourselves groan within ourselves, waiting eagerly for our adoption as sons, the redemption of our body." Romans 8:23

There are times when we are told we have a *positional* standing in Christ. That is true, however, they do not become *actual* in us until we reckon them so in our daily experience.
Soldiers! Take your positions.

> *Heavenly Father, although I will always be your child, from this moment on I take my position as your son or daughter. I will no longer act as a child, being under the bondage of the law and tutors but I will act as a responsible son with all the rights and privileges you have given to me.*

IDENTIFIED IN HIS CIRCUMCISION

He Was Circumcised as Man for Us

"And when eight days were completed before His circumcision, His name was then called Jesus, the Name given by the angel before He was conceived in the womb." Luke 2:21

We Are Circumcised in Him on Our Journey Back to Glory

In His circumcision He was identified with man; in our circumcision we are identified with Him as we put no confidence in the flesh; the flesh has been rendered powerless in Christ. The flesh can be called that part of man, deprived of the Spirit of God, and dominated by sin.

"Therefore consider the members of your earthly body as dead to immorality, impurity, passion, evil desire, and greed, which amounts to idolatry. For it is on account of these things that the wrath of God will come." Colossians 3:5-6

"And in Him you were also circumcised with a circumcision made without hands, in the removal of the body of the flesh by the circumcision of Christ." Colossians 2:11

"For he is not a Jew who is one outwardly; neither is circumcision that which is outward in the flesh. But he is a Jew who is one inwardly; and circumcision is that which is of the heart, by the spirit, not by the letter; and his praise is not from men, but from God." Romans 2:28-29

IDENTIFIED IN WISDOM, STATURE, AND FAVOR

He Increased in Wisdom, Stature and Favor as Man

"He increased in wisdom and in stature, and in favor with God and man." Luke 2:52

"He shall grow up before Him, (the Father) as a tender plant." Isaiah 53:2

We Increase in Wisdom, Stature and Favor in Him on Our Path to Glory

"The path of the righteous is like the light of dawn, which shines brighter and brighter until full day." Proverbs 4:18

"He who began a good work in you will bring it to completion at the day of Jesus Christ." Philippians. 1:6 NKJV

"But by His doing we are in Christ Jesus, who became to us wisdom from God, and righteousness and sanctification, and redemption." 1 Corinthians 1:30

"But the wisdom from above is first pure, then peaceable, gentle, reasonable, full of mercy and good fruits, unwavering, without hypocrisy." James 3:17

"And He gave some as apostles, and some as prophets, and some as evangelists, and some as pastors and teachers, for the equipping of the saints for the work of service, to the building up of the body of Christ; until we all attain to the unity of the faith, and of the knowledge of the Son of God, to a mature man, to the measure of the stature which belongs to the fullness of Christ." Ephesians 4: 11-13

"Therefore, leaving the elementary teaching about the Christ, let us press on to maturity." Hebrews 6:1

"But speaking the truth in love, we are to grow up
in all aspects into Him, who is the head, even Christ."
Ephesians 4:15

He increased in favor with God and man, so we too increase
in favor with God as we are changed more and more into His
likeness. And we increase in favor with man as they see Christ
in us.

IDENTIFIED IN HIS BAPTISM

In His baptism the Son of God, who was God, is God, and
always will be God, became man and was identified as the Son
of Man. In our baptism we who are sons of man are identified
as the sons of God.

Perhaps the question needs to be asked: Why was Jesus
baptized? John's baptism was a baptism of repentance for
forgiveness of sin. (Matt. 3:11, Mark 1:4) Jesus, as the
perfect Lamb of God, had no sin. As you know some things
He did as our *example* and other things He did as our
substitute. Jesus' baptism was done as both our example
and our substitute. As man, the last Adam, His baptism of
repentance was for us as our substitute; He was identified
with man. He also showed us by example that the way to
life is through death.

In His Baptism He Was Identified with Us as Man

And John was preaching and saying, "After me
comes One who is mightier than I, and I am not even
fit to stoop down and untie His sandals. I baptize you
with water; but He will baptize you with the Holy
Spirit." Mark 1:7-8

"Thus, Jesus arrived from Galilee at the Jordan
coming to John to be baptized by him. But John tried
to prevent Him, saying, 'I have need to be baptized by
you, and do you come to me?' But Jesus answering
said to him, 'Permit it at this time; for in this way it

is fitting for us to fulfill all righteousness;' then he permitted Him." Matt. 3:13-15

"John answered and said to them all, "As for me, I baptize you with water; but He who is mightier than I is coming, and I am not fit to untie the thong of His sandals; He Himself will baptize you in the Holy Spirit and fire. 'And His winnowing fork is in His hand to clean out His threshing floor, and to gather the wheat into His barn; but He will burn up the chaff with unquenchable fire.'" Luke 3:16-17

In Our Baptism We Are Identified with Him on Our Path to Glory

In the simplest of explanations water baptism is an outer expression of an inward happening as we are identified with Him in His death, burial and resurrection.

"And corresponding to that, baptism (our identification with Christ in His death, burial and resurrection) now saves you — not the removal of dirt from the flesh, but an appeal to God for a good conscience — through the resurrection of Jesus Christ." 1 Peter 3:21 paraphrased.

"He who has believed (trust in and totally rely on) and has been baptized (identified with Him) shall be saved; but he who has disbelieved shall be condemned." Mark 16:16

"For by one Spirit we were all baptized into one body..." 1 Corinthians 12:13

IDENTIFIED IN HIS MINISTRY

In His Ministry He Was Identified with Us as Man

Everything that Jesus did in His life and ministry on earth He did as man, in total dependence on the Father. He lived His life on earth as God intended man to live, in total dependence on the Father. He was the only normal person to ever walk this earth. He was the perfect man, without sin.

"Have this attitude in yourselves which was also in Christ Jesus, who, although He existed in the form of God, did not regard equality with God a thing to be grasped, but emptied Himself, taking the form of a bond-servant, and being made in the likeness of men. Being found in appearance as a man, He humbled Himself by becoming obedient to the point of death, even death on a cross." Philippians 2:5-9

"Do you not believe that I am in the Father, and the Father is in Me? The words that I say to you I do not speak on My own initiative, but the Father abiding in Me does His works." John 14:10

"Therefore Jesus answered and was saying to them, "Truly, truly, I say to you, the Son can do nothing of Himself, unless it is something He sees the Father doing; for whatever the Father does, these things the Son also does in like manner." John 5:19

"I can do nothing on My own initiative. As I hear, I judge; and My judgment is just, because I do not seek My own will, but the will of Him who sent Me." John 5:30

"Men of Israel, listen to these words: Jesus the Nazarene, a man attested to you by God with miracles and wonders and signs which *God performed* through Him in your midst, just as you yourselves know." Acts 2:22

This brings us to an important question. How did Jesus do what He did? Although being God He laid aside His powers as God and became man. Everything He did on earth He did as man in complete obedience to the Father. See Philippians 2: 6-11.

> "Peace be with you; as the Father has sent Me, so send I you." John 20:21

In Ministry We Are Identified with Him on Our Path to Glory

As the Son walked in total dependence on the Father, so we too must walk by grace, through faith, in total dependence on the Father.

> "...and He died for all, so that they who live might no longer live for themselves, but for Him who died and rose again on their behalf." 2 Corinthians 5:15

> "I am the vine, you are the branches; he who abides in Me and I in him, he bears much fruit, for apart from Me you can do nothing." John 15:5

> "Now all these things are from God, who reconciled us to Himself through Christ, and gave to us the ministry of reconciliation." 2 Corinthians 5:18

> "Namely, that God was in Christ reconciling the world to Himself, not counting their trespass against them, and He has committed to us the word of reconciliation." 2 Corinthians 5:19

> "Therefore, we are ambassadors for Christ, as though God were entreating through us; we beg you on behalf of Christ, be reconciled to God." 2 Corinthians 5:20

> "As you therefore have received Christ Jesus the Lord, so walk in Him." Colossians 2:6

"The one who says he abides in Him ought himself to walk in the same manner as He walked." 1 John 2:6

IDENTIFIED IN HIS CRUCIFIXION
In His Crucifixion He Was Identified with Us as Man

"But now in Christ Jesus you who formerly were far off have been brought near by the blood of Christ." Ephesians 2:13

"And being found in appearance as a man, He humbled Himself by becoming obedient to the point of death, even death on a cross." Philippians 2:8

"Having cancelled out the certificate of debt consisting of decrees against us and which was hostile to us: and He has taken it out of the way, having nailed it to the cross." Colossians 2:14

"...Who for the joy set before Him endured the cross, despising the shame, and has sat down at the right hand of the throne of God," Hebrews 12:2

In His Crucifixion We Are Identified with Him on Our Path to Glory

Since it is impossible for a man to crucify himself we must take His crucifixion as our crucifixion.

"I have been crucified with Christ; and it is no longer I who live, but Christ lives in me; and the life I now live in the flesh I live by faith in the Son of God, who loved me, and delivered himself up for me." Galatians 2:20

"God looks upon us as having died with Christ, and this fact makes possible the triumph of the Christian life." [5]

"Knowing this that our old self was crucified with Him, that our body of sin might be done away with, that we should no longer be slaves to sin: 7 for he who has died is freed from sin." Romans 6: 6-7

"Now those who belong to Christ Jesus have crucified the flesh with its passions and desires." Galatians 5:24

"But may it never be that I should boast, except in the cross of our Lord Jesus Christ, through which the world has been crucified to me, and I to the world." Galatians 6:14

"…And He Himself bore our sins in His body on the cross, that we might die to sin and live to righteousness; for by His wounds you were healed." 1 Peter 2:24

IDENTIFIED IN HIS DEATH
In His Death He Was Identified with Man
Not only did He die *for* sin, but He also died *to* sin.

"For the death that He died, He died to sin, once for all; but the life that He lives, He lives to God." Romans 6:10

"For this reason the Father loves me, because I lay down my life that I may take it again. No one has taken it from me, but I lay it down on my own initiative. I have authority to lay it down, and I have authority to take it up again." John 10:17-18

"For the love of Christ controls us, having concluded this, that one died for all, therefore all died." 2 Corinthians 5:14

"But God demonstrates His own love toward us, in that while we were yet sinners, Christ died for us." Romans 5:8

"Christ died for our sins according to the Scriptures," 1 Corinthians 15:3

"For God has not destined us for wrath, but for obtaining salvation through our Lord Jesus Christ, who died for us, that whether we are awake or asleep, we may live together with Him." 1 Thessalonians 5:9-10

In His Death We Are Identified with Him on Our Path to Glory

In our identification with Him in His death, two basic themes stand out. (1) We are dead to the law. Galatians 2:19, and (2) We are dead to sin. Romans 6:11. And they are both accomplished the same way, through His death. His death has become our death because we are in Him.

"For you have died and your life is hidden with Christ in God." Colossians 3:3

"Even so consider yourselves to be dead to sin, but alive to God in Christ Jesus." Romans 6:11

"I died to the law, that I might live to God." Galatians 2:19

"For the love of Christ controls us, having concluded this, that one died for all, therefore all died." 2 Corinthians 5:14

"How shall we who died to sin still live in it?" Romans 6:2

"Therefore, my brethren, you also were made to die to the Law through the body of Christ, that you might be joined to another, to Him who was raised from the dead, that we might bear fruit for God." Romans 7:4

"But now we have been released from the law, having died to that by which we were bound, so that we serve in newness of the spirit and not in oldness of the letter." Romans 7:6

"Otherwise, what will those do who are baptized (identified with the dead) for the dead? If the dead are not raised at all, why then are they baptized (identified with them) for them?" 1 Corinthians 15:29

"I protest, brethren, by the boasting in you, which I have in Christ Jesus our Lord, I die daily." 1 Corinthians 15:31

• • •

DEAD TO SIN

Do you realize that you cannot battle the flesh with the flesh? You can only battle the flesh with faith. Faith in the finished work of Christ. Galatians 3:3 "Are you so foolish? Having begun by the Spirit, are you now being perfected by the flesh?"

Can you imagine a creator who created our bodies with certain limits and temptations and gave us no power to have victory over them? It would be a very cruel trick. Many Christians feel that the only power they have over the flesh is to try harder to bring the flesh under their control, instead of trusting in the victory we have in the finished work of Jesus Christ.

As a Christian if I told you that Jesus Christ died *for* your sin you would believe it and would have no problem telling me the story of salvation. You would probably tell me how He died for me and paid the penalty of my sin and how He was the sacrifice for my sin. But do you realize that He also died *to* sin.

"For the death He died, He died to sin, once for all:
but the life that He lives, He lives to God." Romans 6:10

Some things Jesus did as our example and other things He did as our substitute. He died to sin one time for everyone. The fact is He died to sin as our substitute. This gives us the victory over the power of sin in our lives. It's important to realize that we were incapable of that death because we were already dead in trespasses and sin.

He died to sin in our place. We are in Christ and Christ is in us. His death became effective on the cross. It became effective in my behavior when I counted it as true in my daily walk. Many times, Paul used the word *reckon* which means to *count as true.*

"Likewise reckon ye also yourselves to be dead indeed unto sin, but alive unto God through Jesus Christ our Lord." Romans 6:11 KJV

"How shall we who died to sin still live in it?" Romans 6:2

"Knowing this that our old self was crucified with Him, that our body of sin might be done away with, that we should no longer be slaves to sin;" Romans 6:6

"For you have died and your life is hidden with Christ in God." Colossians 3:3

"I have been crucified with Christ; and it is no longer I who live, but Christ lives in me; and the life I now live in the flesh I live by faith in the Son of God, who loved me, and delivered himself up for me." Galatians 2:20

"God looks upon us as having died with Christ, and this fact makes possible the triumph of the Christian life." [6]

This victory over sin in the life of a Christian is not attained by some 12-step program. Victory over sin is appropriated through the death, burial and resurrection of Jesus Christ. The death of Christ occurred over 2,000 years ago. It became effective in my behavior when I reckoned it so in my daily behavior.

Sin has not died, it is still very active and all around us. We are to reckon ourselves to be dead to sin.

The old Adamic nature cannot be cured, trained, polished, or cleaned. It can only be crucified with Christ.

We need the victory over the sin in our lives now. We won't need it when we die and go to heaven. There won't be any sin. We can have the victory over sin's power by standing on the finished work of Christ. When we go to heaven we will be delivered from sin's presence as well as its power.

You will discover that after realizing that you are dead to sin you have only come half way. The next step is to reckon on the fact that you are alive unto God through the resurrection of Christ.

IDENTIFIED IN HIS BURIAL
In His Burial He Was Identified with Man

"For I delivered to you as the first importance what I also received, that Christ died for our sins according to the scriptures, and that He was buried, and that He was raised on the third day according to the scriptures." 1 Corinthians 15:3-4

In His Burial We Are Identified with Him on Our Path to Glory

"Therefore we have been buried with Him through baptism into death, in order that as Christ was raised from the dead through the glory of the Father, so we too might walk in newness of life." Romans 6:4

"Having been buried with Him in baptism, in which you were also raised up with Him through faith in the working of God, who raised Him from the dead." Colossians 2:12

Buried with Him

"Therefore we have been buried with Him through baptism into death," Romans 6:4

"Our Identification with the Lord Jesus Christ in His burial is a very important truth, for it teaches that our sin can never again be brought against us." [7]

Columnist Heywood Brown was induced to attend a confession meeting, which was very popular in the 30's. He wrote in his column that, "...at last he had found the type of religion that he could go for in a big way; for the next best thing to committing a sin is telling about it afterward. A pint always becomes a quart in the telling."

Leviticus chapter 16 says beginning in verse 7: "And he shall take the two goats and present them before the Lord at the doorway of the tent of meeting. And Aaron shall cast lots for the two goats, one lot for the Lord and the other lot for the scapegoat. Then Aaron shall offer the goat on which the lot for the Lord fell, and make it a sin offering. But the goat on which the lot for the scapegoat fell shall be presented alive before the Lord, to make atonement upon it, to send it into the wilderness as the scapegoat."

Verse 21-23 "Then Aaron shall lay both his hands on the head of the live goat, and confess over it all the iniquities of the sons of Israel, and all their transgressions in regard to all their sins; and he shall lay them on the head of the goat and send it away into the wilderness by the hand of a man who stand in readiness. And the goat shall bear on itself all their iniquities to a solitary land; and he shall release the goat in the wilderness. Then Aaron shall come into the tent of meeting, and take off the linen garments which he put on when he went into the holy place, and shall leave them there."

"The central feature of Yom Kippur was the special offering of two goats. Aaron presented them before Jehovah at the door of the Tabernacle of the congregation. There he cast lots on the two animals — one for the Lord, the other for the scapegoat. The animal on which the Lord's lot fell was killed as a sin offering, and its blood was applied to the altar and utensils of worship. Then the high priest laid his hands upon the head of the live goat and confessed over him all the iniquities of the people of Israel, all their transgressions and sins were put upon the head of this goat. Finally, the high priest sent the living goat into the wilderness by a special messenger."

"The goat shall bear all their iniquities upon him to a solitary land; and he shall let the goat go in the wilderness." (Lev. 16:22) After this the messenger had to wash his clothes and bathe his body before returning to the camp of God's people.

What a beautiful picture of the work of Christ in redeeming us! First, He bore our sins in His own body on the cross; then He carried them far away so that they can never be charged to us again." [8]

All our sin; past, present and future were put upon Him and He carried them away to the wilderness away from the presence of God. He carried them to hell for us, where they belong.

You may know Jesus as the sacrificial offering for our sin. Do you know Him as the scapegoat, the one who carried our sin away?

The Apostles Creed

"I believe in God the Father Almighty, Creator of heaven and earth.

And in Jesus Christ, His only Son, our Lord; Who was conceived by the Holy Ghost. Born of the Virgin Mary; Suffered under Pontius Pilate. Was crucified, dead and buried; *He descended_into hell*; The third day He rose again from the dead; He ascended into heaven and sitteth on the right hand of God the Father Almighty; From thence He shall come to judge the quick and the dead.

I believe in the Holy Spirit; The holy Christian Church, the communion of saints; The forgiveness of sins; The resurrection of the body; and the Life everlasting. Amen." [9]

• • •

He Took Not Only the Sins You Have Done but Also the Sins Done Against You

What has God done with those sins? They are:
- Forgiven (1John 2:12)
- Forgotten, and Cleansed (Jeremiah 33:8)
- Gone and Atoned for (Romans 5:11)
- Covered (Psalm 32:1)
- Cast into the depths of the sea (Micah 7:19)
- Removed as far as the East is from the West (Psalm 103:12)
- Blotted out as a thick cloud (Isaiah 44:22)
- Cast behind God's back (Isaiah 38:17)
- and Remembered against us no more (Jeremiah 31:34) —Barnhouse [10]

You Have No Right to Remember What God Forgets

Satan accuses us before the Father day and night, he is the accuser of the brethren. Revelation 12:10 He knows what sins were done because they were taken to hell and buried by Christ. Satan is the one who wants to keep bringing them up before the Father. We have an advocate with the Father, Jesus Christ, "He liveth to make intercession for them." Hebrews 7:25 KJV

You may believe that you have been *put on the shelf* due to some past sin. That sin was put on Christ and is remembered against you no more —leave it there.

"And they overcame him because of the blood of the Lamb and because of the word of their testimony, and they did not love their life even to death." Revelation 12:11

Is there something you need to bury with Christ, so you can live the life He intended for you to live? The enemy is the one who wants to keep bringing these things up; not the Lord — they have been buried with Christ.

He made proclamation of victory over sin, the price has been paid; our sin was taken to hell and left there.

"...in which also He went and made proclamation to the spirits now in prison," 1 Peter 3:19

"For this gospel has for this purpose been preached even to those who are dead, that though they are judged in the flesh as men, they may live in the spirit according to the will of God." 1 Peter 4:6

If the enemy wants to bring up your past sins against you, you may ignore him or tell him that Jesus already took that accusation for you, and it has been forgiven.

IDENTIFIED IN HIS RESURRECTION
In His Resurrection He Is Identified with Us
His resurrection proves that the sacrifice of Himself was accepted.

"And God raised Him up again, putting an end to the agony of death, since it was impossible for Him to be held in its power." Acts 2:24

"...wait for His son from heaven, whom He raised from the dead, that is Jesus, who delivers us from the wrath to come." 1 Thessalonians 1:10

"For the death He died, He died to sin, once for all; but the life that He lives, He lives to God." Romans 6:10

"For He was foreknown before the foundation of the world, but has appeared in these last times for the sake of you who through Him are believers in God, who raised Him from the dead and gave Him glory, so that your faith and hope are in God." 1 Peter 1:20-21

In His Resurrection We Are Identified in Him on Our Path to Glory

"If you then have been raised up with Christ, keep seeking the things above where Christ is seated, at the right hand of God." Colossians 3:1

"And He died for all, that they who live should no longer live for themselves but for Him who died and rose again on their behalf." 2 Corinthians 5:15

"But God, being rich in mercy, because of His great love with which He loved us, even when we were dead in our transgressions, made us alive together with Christ (by grace you have been saved), and raised us up with Him, and seated us with Him in the heavenly places, in Christ Jesus," Ephesians 2:4-6

"Having been buried with Him in baptism, in which you were also raised up with Him through faith in the working of God, who raised Him from the Dead." Colossians 2:12

"Even so consider yourselves to be dead to sin, but alive to God in Christ Jesus." Romans 6:11

IDENTIFIED IN HIS LIFE
In His Life He Was Identified with Us

"God has sent His only begotten Son into the world so that we might live through Him." 1John 4:9

"And the witness is this, that God has given us eternal life, and this life is in His son." 1 John 5:11

"For God so loved the world that He gave His only begotten Son, that whoever believes in Him should not perish, but have eternal life." John 3:16

In Our Life We Are Identified with Him on Our Path to Glory
The death He died qualifies us for the life He lives.

"For if while we were enemies, we were reconciled to God through the death of His son, much more, having been reconciled, we shall be saved by His life." Romans 5:10

He came to give dead men what they needed and that was life. Jesus came to give us life. The life of all flesh is in the blood. His death paid the price, so we can be saved by His life. Without His death we would not have His life. His life has now become our life, without Him we would not have life.

"The life that I now live in the flesh I live by faith in the Son of God." Galatians 2:20

"And the witness is this, that God has given us eternal life, and this life is in His Son, He who has the Son has the life; he who does not have the Son of God does not have the life." 1 John 5:11-12

"Now He is not the God of the dead, but of the living for all live to Him." Luke 20:38

114

"For God did not send the Son into the world to judge the world; but that the world should be saved through Him." John 3:17

"Truly, truly I say to you, he who hears my word, and believes Him who sent me, has eternal life, and does not come into judgment, but has passed out of death into life." John 5:24

"Therefore if any man is in Christ, he is a new creature; the old things passed away; behold new things have come." 2 Corinthians 5:17

"For to me, to live is Christ, and to die is gain." Philippians 1:21

"He who has the Son has the life; he who does not have the Son of God does not have life." 1 John 5:12

"For the law of the spirit of life in Christ Jesus has set you free from the law of sin and of death." Romans 8:2

Saved By His Life

You have been saved from the *penalty* of sin by His sacrificial death. You are being saved from the *power* of sin by His life. One day I will be saved from the *presence* of sin by His blood. His death has enabled you to be saved by His life. He gave His life so that we could share His life.

"But this He spoke of the Spirit, whom those who believed in Him were to receive; for the Spirit was not yet given, because Jesus was not yet glorified." John 7:39

What needed to happen before the outpouring of the Holy Spirit? Did His death allow for the outpouring of the Holy Spirit? No! Did His resurrection allow Him to release the

Holy Spirit? No! His death & resurrection qualified Him to be glorified.

> "And gathering them together, He commanded them not to leave Jerusalem, but to wait for what the Father had promised. 'Which,' He said, 'you heard of from Me; for John baptized with water, but you shall be baptized with the Holy Spirit, not many days from now'." Acts 1:4-5

The disciples were ordered to wait until they received what the Father had promised. The Holy Spirit could not be given until Jesus was glorified. They patiently waited in the upper room; days had passed and then weeks. The disciple's family members would come to them, bring them food and ask; "What are you doing here? Don't you know that you should be fishing and providing for your families?" And still they waited because Jesus told them to wait. In fact, He told them "don't do anything until you receive what the Father had promised." They didn't know what they were waiting for or what it would look like when they saw it. But still they waited. Maybe they missed it, they thought. Weeks became a month, and it wasn't until 50 days had passed that the promise was given. Instantly they knew that Jesus Was Glorified! The outpouring of the Holy Spirit was proof that *Jesus was glorified.*

> "Men of Israel, why do you marvel at this, or why do you gaze at us, as if by our own power or piety we had made him walk? The God of Abraham, Isaac, and Jacob, the God of our Fathers, has glorified His Servant Jesus," Acts 3:12-13

> "Therefore having been exalted to the right hand of God, and having received from the Father the promise of the Holy Spirit, He has poured forth this which you both see and hear." Acts 2:33

His death and resurrection have qualified us to be glorified in Him. His glorification has become our glorification. What is the pre-requisite for you to receive the baptism (identification) of the Holy Spirit?

Jesus Was Glorified, And He Lives in You

"Christ in you the hope of Glory." Colossians 1:27

"But you shall receive power when the Holy Spirit has come upon you; and you shall be My witnesses both in Jerusalem, and in all Judea and Samaria, and even to the remotest part of the earth." Acts 1:8

We Will Be Witnesses of Him

He who honors the Son honors the Father also.

And Peter said to them, "Repent, and let each of you be baptized in the Name of Jesus Christ for the forgiveness of your sins; and you shall receive the gift of the Holy Spirit. For the promise is for you and your children, and for all who are far off, as many as the Lord our God shall call to Himself." Acts 2:38-39

His Death and Resurrection Have Qualified Us to Be Glorified in Him

He died for us so that He could live His life in us. We are saved by His life.

"For if while we were enemies we were reconciled to God through the death of His Son, much more, having been reconciled, we shall be saved by His life." Romans 5:10

"But when He, the Spirit of truth, comes, He will guide you into all the truth; for He will not speak on His own initiative, but whatever He hears, He will speak; and He will disclose to you what is to come. *He shall glorify Me; for He shall take of Mine, and shall disclose it to you.*" John 16:13-14

"Any teaching which detracts from the centrality of Christ under the pretense of leading men to maturity and perfection is a perversion that threatens the very essence of the Christian Faith. The book of Colossians makes anathema any belief or practice that displaces the centrality of Jesus as redeemer and the perfecter of His people." [11]

> *He is in us...Christ in us! Greater is He that is in us than he that is in the world...Jesus Christ is our hope of glory. Though He was dead...He is alive! Though He was buried...He is risen! Though He seemed defeated...He is victorious! And He is in us. Thank you Father that He is in us. We are in Him...We've been chosen in the Lord before the foundations of the world...we've obtained an inheritance in Him. And...you have seated us together in* Heavenly *places in Him. How awe inspiring is this work of salvation. We are in Him. How uplifting and encouraging are your words O Lord. We thank you so much that He is in us and we are in Him! (Prayer by John Hayes)*

• • •

IDENTIFIED IN HIS RIGHTEOUSNESS
He Was Made Righteous for Us

This is the name by which He will be called, "The Lord our righteousness." Jeremiah 23:6

"For as through the one man's disobedience the many were made sinners, even so through the obedience of the one the many will be made righteous." Romans 5:19

"And if anyone sins, we have an Advocate with the Father, Jesus Christ the righteous." 1 John 2:1

"If you know that He is righteous, you know that everyone also who practices righteousness is born of Him." 1 John 2:29

His Righteousness Has Become Our Righteousness

Originally righteousness meant "the state of him who is such as he ought to be." That which cannot be *attained* may be *obtained* as a gift. We cannot come to Him holding up our own righteousness we don't have any apart from Him. To be normal is to be in the "state of him who is such as he ought to be." Be the person God created you to be.

"There is none righteous, not even one." Romans 3:10

"For if by the transgression of the one, death reined through the one, much more those who receive the abundance of grace and the gift of righteousness will reign in life through the one, Jesus Christ." Romans 5:17

His righteousness has become our righteousness. I do not do things to become righteous, because I am righteous I do those things.

"He made Him who knew no sin to be sin on our behalf that we might become the righteousness of God in Him." 2 Corinthians 5:21

"And if Christ is in you, though the body is dead because of sin, yet the spirit is alive because of righteousness." Romans 8:10

"But now apart from the Law the righteousness of God has been manifested, being witnessed by the Law and the Prophets; even the righteousness of God through faith in Jesus Christ for all those who believe." Romans 3:21,22

"...that as sin reigned in death, even so grace might reign through righteousness to eternal life through Jesus Christ our Lord." Romans 5:21

He is the righteous one, not me, and I can only come to the Father through His righteousness. If I come to the Father holding up my own righteousness, He will inspect it and find it wanting.

"But the righteous man shall live by faith." Romans 1:17

"The prayer of a righteous man availeth much." James 5:16 NKJV

"For as through the one man's disobedience the many were made sinners, even so through the obedience of the One the many will be made righteous." Romans 5:19

"...that, in reference to your former manner of life, you lay aside the old self, which is being corrupted in accordance with the lusts of deceit, and that you be renewed in the spirit of your mind, and put on the new self, which in the likeness of God has been created in righteousness and holiness of the truth." Ephesians 4:22-24

"Stand firm therefore, having girded your loins with truth, and having put on the breastplate of righteousness, ..." Ephesians 6:14

"If we confess our sin, He is faithful and righteous to forgive us our sins and to cleanse us from all unrighteousness." 1 John 1:9

• • •

OBEDIENCE = APPROPRIATION

Every aspect of His life on earth was for us. He gave His life *for* us, but He also gave His life *to* us.

Somehow, we think that God put us on earth to struggle and try to do His will and laughs at us when we get it wrong.

"Grace and peace be multiplied to you in the knowledge of God and of Jesus our Lord; seeing that His divine power has granted to us everything pertaining to life and godliness, through the true knowledge of Him who called us by His own glory and excellence." 2 Peter 1:2-3

Suppose a woman and her young son are getting ready to go to church. She dresses her son and tells him to wait on the porch until she finishes getting dressed. Her son walks out the back door as he waits for his mother. He steps off the porch and slips and falls in the mud as he catches himself with his hands. Knowing that he needed to stay clean he tries to clean his hands by wiping them on his clothes. In our efforts to clean ourselves we simply make matters worse. The Lord Jesus is the only one who can clean us and make us fit for the Kingdom of God.

If you've been a Christian, if even for a short time, you know that we have three enemies: the devil, the world and our own flesh.

When counteracting our enemy, the devil, you can cast him out in the power of Jesus Christ, stand firm, or flee.

When counteracting the world or the flesh, you look at the finished work of Christ and you reckon yourself as having died with Him.

"For you have died and your life is hidden with Christ in God." Colossians 3:3

"Knowing this, that our old self was crucified with Him, that our body of sin might be done away with, that we should no longer be slaves to sin." Romans 6:6
"Now those who belong to Christ Jesus have crucified the flesh with its passions and desires." Galatians 5:24

"But may it never be that I would boast, except, in the cross of the Lord Jesus Christ, through which the world has been crucified to me, and I to the world." Galatians 6:14

If you struggle and try to overcome the deeds of the world or your own flesh under your own power, then, if you're able to somehow accomplish it, all glory goes to you. But if you reckon on the fact that you died with Christ then all glory goes to Him.

It has been said that I have two lions dwelling in me, a good lion and a bad lion. Which one is the strongest? The one I feed the most.

"In my flesh dwelleth no good thing." Romans 7:18 KJV

The flesh cannot be fixed up, patched up, painted or repaired —it is only worthy of death.

"But Jesus on His part, was not entrusting Himself to them, for He knew all men, and because He did not need any one to bear witness concerning men, for He Himself knew what was in man." John 2:24-25

Jesus said; "For out of the heart come evil thoughts, murders, adulteries, fornications, thefts, false witness, slanders. These are the things which defile the man; but to eat with unwashed hands does not defile the man." Matthew 15:19-20

We need to be careful that we do not turn our faith into a mental exercise. You might be able to change your mind about a few things, but only the Lord has the power to change your heart. King David prayed: "Create in me a clean heart, O God, and renew a steadfast spirit within me." Psalms 51:10

Due to our past relationship with the law we believe that when we sin we will be punished. This is known as the "law of sin and death." Another law has been instituted in Christ; this is known as the law of "the Spirit of life in Christ Jesus."

"For the law of the Spirit of life in Christ Jesus has set you free from the law of sin and of death. For what the law could not do, weak as it was through the flesh, God did; sending His own son in the likeness of sinful flesh and as an offering for sin, He condemned sin in the flesh, in order that the requirement of the law might be fulfilled in us, who do not walk according to the flesh, but according to the Spirit." Romans 8:2-4

There are times when we choose to sin, and we expect to be punished, but I assure you it's much worse than that; we come short of His glory. "For all have sinned and come short of the glory of God." Romans 3:23 KJV

A Christian isn't looking for a loophole in the law so that he can sin; he is looking for deliverance from the power of sin over his life.

We have the privilege of knowing our identity in Christ not by struggling to obey but by appropriation of the finished work of Christ.

"You shall know the truth and the truth shall make you free." John 8:32

The bodies that we have right now are called mortal bodies (subject to death), when we die and go to heaven we will have immortal bodies (not subject to death).

"But if the Spirit of Him who raised Jesus from the dead dwells in you, He who raised Christ Jesus from the dead will also give life to your mortal bodies through His Spirit who indwells you." Romans 8:11

He died for us so that He could live His life in us. We are saved by His life. "For if while we were enemies we were reconciled to God through the death of His Son, much more, having been reconciled, we shall be saved by His life." Romans 5:10

• • •

GOOD

"In the beginning God created the heavens and the earth." Genesis 1:1 The phrase, "...and God saw that it was *good*." is stated five times in Genesis one, and then, "God saw all that He had made and behold it was *very good*." Genesis 1:31.

It was created to be good, "un-mixed good." The good was not contaminated with evil, it was un-mixed. When sin came into the world due to Adams fall, the good became contaminated, good became mixed.

"Therefore, just as through one man sin entered into the world, and death through sin, and so death spread to all men, because all sinned." Romans 5:12

Paul said,

"For that which I am doing, I do not understand; for I am not practicing what I would like to do, but I am doing the very thing I hate. But if I do the very thing I do not wish to do, I agree with the law, confessing that it is good. So now, no longer am I the one doing it, but sin which indwells me. For I know that nothing good dwells in me, that is, in my flesh, for the wishing is present in me, but the doing of the good is not. For the good that I wish, I do not do; but I practice the very evil that I do not wish. But if I am doing the very thing I do not wish, I am no longer the one doing it, but sin which dwells in me. I find then the principle that evil is present in me, the one who wishes to do good." Romans 7:15-21

Paul was, as we are, seeking for good without corruption. He was seeking for un-contaminated good, un-mixed good. When I built my cabin, I had a well digger come in, and He drilled down 350-feet and hit what is considered good water. To all outward appearances it was good. When we did a test on the water we discovered that it was contaminated with iron, trace amounts of magnesium and other minerals as well as trace amounts of bacteria. It was good enough for consumption, but it was still contaminated. I'm sure you've heard of "Pure Rocky Mountain Spring Water"; guess what, it's contaminated. In our world today, there is no such thing as pure good due to sin coming upon the earth.

No matter how good you are, you're corrupt. No matter how good your spouse is, he/she is corrupt. No matter how good your health is, it's corrupt. No matter how good your church is, it's corrupt. No matter how good your prayers are, they're corrupt. No matter how good your pastor is, he's corrupt. I know a guy who's good at wood work and he seeks perfection, but no matter how hard he tries his finished product is corrupt. Another seeks to be a good Bible teacher, and no matter how much he studies and how much he prays his teaching is still contaminated.

"Wretched man that I am; Who will set me free from the body of this death? Thanks be to God through Jesus Christ our Lord!" Romans 7:24-25

"The anxious longing of the creation waits eagerly for the revealing of the sons of God. For the creation was subjected to futility, not of its own will, but because of Him who subjected it, in hope that the creation itself also will be set free from its slavery to corruption into the freedom of the glory of the children of God, for we know that the whole creation groans and suffers the pains of childbirth together until now." Romans 8:19-22

It's a good thing when you become discouraged about how things are in this world. You should be. We're not home yet! One day we will be with the Lord where there will be eternal, un-mixed good; until that time, we have a job to do and that is to allow the Good One to do His work through us.

No longer do you need to prove to me or others how good you are. No longer do you need to prove to God how good you are. Without Jesus in your life you are hopelessly, completely destitute and totally corrupt. Unless you realize this, you will have no need of a Savior.

> "In my flesh dwelleth no good thing." Romans 7:18 KJV

Jesus did not come to patch up your old nature, it's not worth patching up. He came to make all things new.

> "Do not put new wine into old wineskins, they would both be ruined." Mark 2:22 KJV

> "If any man is in Christ, he is a new creature; the old things passed away, behold new things have come." 2 Corinthians 5:17.

It is not a problem that there is so much darkness and corruption in this world. The real problem is there is not enough light. The light overcomes the darkness.

> "Jesus, the light of the world, came in the darkness and the darkness could not overpower Him." John 1:5

Jesus was not afraid of the dark, and neither should we. The amazing thing is that God has chosen to do His work through us, as corrupt as we are. It's good that you're seeking that which is perfect, but perfection cannot be found on this earth, only in the person of the Lord Jesus Christ.

IDENTIFIED IN HIS CHURCH
In His Church He Is Identified with Us

> "That He might present to Himself the church in all her glory, having no spot or wrinkle or any such thing; but that she should be holy and blameless." Ephesians 5:27

"...Christ loved the church and gave himself up for her; ..." Ephesians 5:25

"He is also head of the body, the church; and He is the beginning, the first-born from the dead; so that He Himself might come to have first place in everything." Colossians 1:18

In His Church We Are Identified with Him on Our Path to Glory

The church is not an organization but an organism.

"And when they had arrived and gathered the church together, they began to report all things that God had done with them..." Acts 14:27

"For God, who said, 'Light shall shine out of darkness,' is the One who has shone in our hearts to give the light of the knowledge of the glory of God in the face of Christ." 2 Corinthians 4:6

"And even if our gospel is veiled, it is veiled to those who are perishing, in whose case the god of this world has blinded the minds of the unbelieving, that they might not see the light of the gospel of the glory of Christ, who is the image of God." 2 Corinthians 4:3-4

• • •

We've just touched upon our identity in Christ, and we learned who He is in us and who we are in Him. We learned that our true identity can only be found in Him. As we grow in Him we are being changed from glory to glory. We are now anxious to see our world touched *for* Christ: but this can only happen when our world is touched *by* Christ. The divine revelation of the presence of God in this world can only be accomplished by God Himself. He has chosen to reveal Himself to the world through His people. He's not trying to hide Himself. He's trying to reveal Himself to the world through His people, as He revealed Himself to the world through His Son. This revelation of Himself to the world is commonly known as *revival*. We are in desperate need of His presence to be manifested in and through us. We need revival.

Just to use the word revive is an admission that something that was once vibrant and alive is now weak or dead and in need of coming alive. That which was once whole is now sick. The only one who is capable of giving life to the dead is the One who is alive.

"Wilt Thou not Thyself revive us again, that Thy people may rejoice in Thee?" Psalm 85:6 KJV

THE REAL FAITH

As the life of the flesh is in the blood, Leviticus 17:11, so faith is the life that flows into the roots.

A tree does not and cannot produce life. The tree is the carrier of the life flowing through its branches. The roots are not the life, they are the carrier that transports life into the tree. The roots can produce nothing without the life. The life is in the nourishment traveling to the roots to cause the tree to grow and produce fruit. The tree does not need to struggle or try to produce life; it cannot do it, only the life flowing through the tree can produce life. You are not the life, you are a carrier of the life produced by the One who said, "I am the way the truth and the life." John14:6 Real Faith is the life that flows into the roots. The roots do not produce the life, but the life produces and nourishes the roots. It is the life that is flowing into the roots that is known as the real faith. You can never struggle or try hard enough to produce life. The life can only be produced by the One who is Life. "Jesus is the author and perfecter of our faith." (Hebrews 12:2)

Living water gives life; life giving water. "…but whoever drinks of the water that I shall give him shall never thirst; but the water that I shall give him shall become in him a well of water springing up to eternal life." John 4:14. Your mind cannot create life. Have we reduced faith to nothing more than an exercise in the metaphysical? Nowhere in the Bible does it tell you that you need to try harder. Somehow, we think we have the ability to help God. We can hinder the working of God in our lives, but we can't help Him.

If it were possible to attain faith for the task by our own struggling and trying to believe, then all glory would go to us. Have we substituted belief and trust for real faith? You say you believe, and that's fine, but the "devils also believe and tremble." The demons trust in and totally rely on Jesus Christ for eternal damnation. *We trust in and totally rely on Jesus Christ for eternal life.*

Faith is either a Fruit of the Spirit, (Galatians 5:22) or a Gift of the Spirit, (1 Corinthians12:9). Love, joy, peace, patience are all fruit of the Spirit given to us by grace through faith. Why do you struggle to have faith when it too is a gift given to us by grace through faith? The faith of God is imparted to man for the need of the moment.

Can you imagine a branch struggling and trying to produce life when out of its innermost being it flows naturally when needed? In Him is Life. You tell me you have faith; I would ask, "Where did you get it?"

Ephesians 6 tells us to take up the full armor of God, (His armor), having girded your loins with truth, (His truth). Put on the breastplate of righteousness, (His righteousness) and having shod your feet with the preparation of the gospel of peace, (His gospel, His peace) in addition to all take up the shield of faith, (His faith) and the helmet of salvation, (His salvation) and the sword of the Spirit, (His sword) which is the word of God. *When you put on His armor the enemy sees God.*

Faith for salvation was given to you as a gift. Ephesians 2:8 "For by grace you have been saved through faith; and that not of yourselves, it is the gift of God."

"As you therefore have received Christ Jesus the Lord, (by grace through faith) so walk in Him, (by grace through faith)." Colossians 2:6 —His Faith!

Heavenly Father; forgive me for struggling and trying to produce faith that can only come from you. You are the One who is working in us both to will and to do of Your good pleasure. You are the author and finisher of our faith. I trust You to be faithful to give us the faith we need for the need of the moment. Thank You for blessing us with Your presence and for allowing Jesus Christ to live His life through us. In Jesus Name, Amen.

REST

The word *rest* holds with it the root of, *calming of the winds*: calm and patient expectation.

He Himself is our peace; He serves and reigns as the Prince of Peace.

"There remains therefore a Sabbath rest for the people of God. For the one who has entered His rest has himself also rested from his works, as God did from His. Let us therefore be diligent to enter that rest, lest anyone fall through following the same example of disobedience." Hebrews 4:9-11 (disobedience can be called a lack of appropriation, or unbelief.)

We cannot refuse to enter the Land of Promise, the place of our promised inheritance, due to our unbelief.

It is not our job to struggle to *hang on to Him*, instead, we are to *trust Him* to *hang on to us*.

He said; "I will never leave you or forsake you." Hebrews 13:5 "For it is God who is at work in you, both to will and to work for His good pleasure." Phil. 2:13

LET HIM! "The Lord is faithful, and He will strengthen and protect you from the evil one." 2 Thessalonians 3:3 He showed Himself strong enough to bring you out of darkness, don't you think He's strong enough to keep you and protect you from the evil one? LET HIM! He is our strength and protector.

We have been on quite a journey as we have sought to learn our identity in Christ and His identity in us. He has led us up the pathway to His glory. The Glory of His Presence. Christ in you the hope of glory.

We have learned to "destroy speculations and every lofty thing raised up against the knowledge of God, and we are taking every thought captive to the obedience of Christ." 2 Corinthians 10:5 We have learned that our life is hidden with Christ in God.

We have learned that everything He did on earth, He did for us. The thing that we have sought has been found in Him. He is our life and our identity. Our weapons of choice are worship and praise as we put our faith and trust in Him and His finished work.

On our journey we have learned that in Him I am justified, redeemed, sanctified, delivered, protected, dead to sin and alive to God. In Him I am made righteous, forgiven, and I have eternal life. This is just the beginning of our path to glory, we have received the down payment, there's more to come. May the Lord continue to bless you on the path that He has chosen for you —the path of Glory.

The Glory of Man
Section Four

Glory In Revival

GLORY IN REVIVAL

What does revival look like? In the United States in 1857-1858 we had the Great Awakening. It began in downtown New York with one man, Jeremiah Lamphier, and a one-hour noon prayer meeting. The first day, September 23, 1857, he prayed alone for half an hour, then four others from different denominations joined him. The next week 40 attended, the week after that 100, including many unsaved. Soon thousands began praying in their church services and in their homes.

Wesley Duewal wrote: "The three rooms at the Fulton Street Church were filled beyond capacity, and hundreds had to go to other places. By early February a nearby Methodist Church was opened, and it immediately overflowed, its balconies were filled with ladies. By March 19th a theater opened for prayer, and half an hour before time to begin, people were turned away. Hundreds stood outside in the streets because they could not get inside. By the end of March over six-thousand people met daily in prayer gathering in New York City. Many churches added evening services for prayer. Soon there were 150 united prayer meetings across Manhattan and Brooklyn." [1]

Almost simultaneously noon prayer meetings sprang up all across America, in Boston, Baltimore, Washington, D.C., Richmond, Charleston, Savannah, Mobile, New Orleans, Vicksburg, Memphis, St. Louis, Pittsburgh, Cincinnati, Chicago, and in a multitude of other cities, towns, and in rural areas. By the end of the fourth month, prayer fervor burned intensely across the nation. It was an awesome demonstration of the sovereign working of the Holy Spirit, and the eager obedience of God's people.

All the people wanted was a place to pray. Sinners would come and ask for prayer. Someone would individually pray for them, and in minutes the newly saved person was rejoicing in Christ. In some towns, nearly the entire population became saved.

The spirit of prayer occupied the land, as though the church had suddenly discovered its power. The majority of the churches in most denominations experienced a new dimension of prayer. The Presbyterian magazine reported that as of May there had been fifty thousand converts of the revival. By February, a New York Methodist magazine reported a total of eight thousand conversions in meetings in one week. The Louisville daily paper reported seventeen thousand Baptist conversions in three weeks during the month of March. And according to a June statement, the conversion figures were at 96,216 — and still counting. All but two of the youth in one high school were saved. A similar event took place in Toledo, Ohio. These are just brief examples of what was happening constantly all across the nation.

A canopy of holy and awesome revival influence — in reality the presence of the Holy Spirit — seemed to hang like an invisible cloud over many parts of the United States, especially over the eastern seaboard. At times this cloud of God's presence even seemed to extend out to sea. Those on ships approaching the east coast at times felt a solemn, holy influence, even one hundred miles away, without even knowing what was happening in America.

Revival began aboard one ship before it reached the coast. People on board began to feel the presence of God and a sense of their own sinfulness. The Holy Spirit convicted them, and they began to repent as the ship neared the harbor. The captain signaled, "Send a minister." Another small commercial ship was heading to port with the captain, and every member of the crew converted in the last 150 miles. Ship after ship arrived with the same story. Both passengers and crews were suddenly convicted of sin and turned to the Lord before they reached the American coast.

The battleship North Carolina was anchored in New York harbor as a naval receiving ship. More than a thousand young men were on board. Four Christians agreed to meet together for prayer and kneeled on the lower deck. The Spirit of God so filled their hearts with joy that they broke into song. Ungodly sailors on the top deck heard the singing, looked down, and saw the boys kneeling. They began running down the ladders mocking and jeering. The convicting power of the Holy Spirit so gripped them that by the time they reached the bottom deck they fell on their knees and began crying for mercy.

Strong men, who were deep in sin, were broken down by the Spirit's power and knelt humbly in prayer and faith. Night after night the sailors prayed, and hundreds were converted on the ship. Ministers were sent for, and they came out from shore to help in the gracious work of the Spirit. The battleship became a mighty center of revival. Converts of the movement, completing their periods of training, were sent to other navy ships. Wherever they went revival fires were kindled in other naval vessels.

The following excerpts were taken from *The Great Awakening of 1857-1858.* [2]

As the noontime prayer meetings increased, attended predominately by the male workers of the cities, the effect was tremendous. Many ministers began having nightly services in which to lead men to Christ. A chain reaction of church after church began to hold morning, afternoon, and evening meetings for both prayer and the counseling of those concerned about their souls.

The same scenes were soon reported from all over the nation, from New York to California, Florida to Maine. It affected judges and college students, businessmen and housewives. At times, schools had to close in order to pray and seek God.

Though it peaked in 1858, it did not stop there. Throughout the Civil War, camps had great revival meetings; over 150,000 were converted in the

Confederate army alone. It also crossed the oceans. In Britain, close to a million people joined the churches due to the revival that swept that land.

This revival was a layman's revival. Though ministers helped to counsel people, it was the laypeople that carried it.

Charles Finney tells of a traveler in a Boston prayer meeting who got up and said: "I am from Omaha the capital of Nebraska. On my journey east, I have found a continuous prayer meeting all the way. We call it about two thousand miles from Omaha to Boston; and there was a prayer meeting about two thousand miles in extent."

Churches benefited greatly from the Revival. At its peak, there was an estimated 50,000 converts per week. During a two-year period, 10,000 were joining churches weekly, and Sunday schools flourished.

The Awakening brought over one million new converts into the American Church, and revived the over four million members present before the Revival. The new life within the churches was shown most dramatically by the resurgence of evangelism.

The famous D.L. Moody began his ministry during the Revival, yet he was never ordained. Even though he founded a Bible college and pastured churches, he always remained a layman.

It wasn't only the churches which benefited from the Awakening. Businessmen began to pay off honest debts, and places of debauchery and taverns by the hundreds closed down. There was also an increased concern in helping the needy and destitute, with great growth in volunteer work, and the financing of the work.

The word I keep hearing from many is "Get Ready."

• • •

*The springs begin in the mountains
and the waters flow downhill, soon becoming
a trickle, then a stream, then a river,
then a wider river until it covers the whole land
and flows into the ocean.*

The above statement is what's happening in our country right now. This is how we got there, and what it means.

The story begins in South Korea and involves Mr. Taechin Kim and Dr. James Hwang. Dr. Hwang is an oncologist from Seoul, who has a calling on his life. Taechin Kim or TC, as he is affectionately known, lived in a small town about an hour away from Seoul, where he returned after working many years for Otis Elevator Company in Singapore as a marketing director. TC knew of Dr. Hwang through newspaper columns the Dr. wrote weekly for national newspapers but had never met him.

TC left Otis Elevator due to an airline malfunction that really woke him up. He was on an airplane leaving Singapore when the alarms in the plane went off after they left the ground. The speakers on the plane kept repeating, "Emergency! Emergency!" TC knew it was an important wakeup call, and all the people on the plane thought they were probably going to crash. He knew he was facing death and wanted more time to devote his life to the Lord and His work. After much difficulty the plane landed. TC knew he was given more time to seek the Lord and devote his life to do His work on the earth. TC was ashamed for how he had lived his life up until that time. He knew he had to make a change. He repented as he was given another opportunity to make his life count for the Lord. As he prayed, he asked if he could serve the Lord in the United States.

When TC returned to his home in Korea, he wanted to meet Dr. Hwang who was pastor of a church in Seoul. He drove the hour it took to get to his church on a Sunday morning; as he was late he sat in the back of the church. While Dr Hwang was preaching he abruptly stopped preaching and asked the congregation to pair up and pray. TC didn't know anybody in the congregation other than Dr. Hwang and didn't know who to pray with. Dr. Hwang walked up to TC and asked him to pray with him. Later that week Dr. Hwang arranged for a meeting with TC, and he and a couple of elders drove the hour to TC's house to meet with him. Dr. Hwang wanted TC and his wife to join his church. They were so honored to have the elders and Dr. Hwang meet with them that they joined their church and thus began a long friendship.

Dr. Hwang is the founder of a missionary medical support ministry called Loving Concern International. He asked TC to head up this organization in Los Angeles, California, which organized medical missionary teams in Bolivia serving four major cities. His job was to organize teams of doctors and nurses and provide medicine, tools and funds to thousands of doctors who were used to help their own people.

In 2006 Dr. Hwang met with Louis Bush and a hundred other people in Korea to found the Transform Korea movement. They held a conference in Seoul in January of that year. Many key speakers from the USA asked the Korean church to pray for the USA. The Korean people had been helped through the years by missionaries coming to help them in Korea, and these Korean Christians now wanted to come to the United States and return the favor of prayer since they could see that our country needed prayer to return to the Lord. They contacted TC in Los Angeles and asked him if he could be the national coordinator for Transform USA. Dr. Hwang suggested the need for Transform USA and chose Colorado Springs due to the leading of the Lord and the many Christian organizations that were headquartered there. They held a three-day conference at the Mayflower Hotel in Denver with about 100 prayer leaders from all faiths in attendance. At that time TC was chosen as national facilitator for Transform USA.

After receiving word from the Lord, Dr. Hwang moved to Colorado Springs with his wife and kids and bought two houses, one to be used as their home and the other as a headquarters building for the ministry. TC and his family moved to Colorado

Springs and bought a house shortly thereafter. Thus, Transform USA was begun.

Many of us have been praying at Transform USA with TC Kim and Dr. Hwang since July of 2007. We meet every Wednesday for about three hours and pray for our country, our churches, schools and educational systems, the media, our military, entertainment venues and leaders. As TC and Dr. Hwang have been called to Colorado Springs and pray, so have many others from around the world. We've had people whom God has called from Korea, China, Hungary, Romania, Mexico, Guatemala, Costa Rica, Nepal, South America, Ethiopia, Syria, Australia, Japan and Pakistan among others. It is so humbling to see these people come from other countries to pray for us when we need it so badly.

We all knew that God had something planned and was preparing us for something, but we didn't know what. We just obeyed and kept praying. When people would ask me, "Why do you go every week to Transform USA and pray?" My answer was: "I don't know. All I know is the Lord asked me to." Many of the people who came could not speak English, so they prayed in their native languages. The Lord drew us together with a love that was unspeakable and full of glory. After three years, He began to reveal His plan a little at a time. The word He began to reveal was "Revival." The command was "Get Ready."

• • •

The event of "One Voice in the Rockies" was held on June 6-7, 2011. This was done to gather a mighty army to battle against the spiritual strongholds of the Pikes Peak Region. We had prayer teams that went to 16 different locations in Colorado, plus a helicopter with prayer warriors flying overhead. At noon on June 6th all the teams blew the shofar at the same time.

On June 6th during the evening after the event, 120 of us gathered at the Boulder Street Church for praise and worship. A homeless man was walking past the church with a broken hand that was swollen and nasty looking. One of our prayer warriors asked him to come into the church. As the homeless man crossed the threshold of the church his hand was instantly healed without anyone touching him or praying for him. He began running up and down the aisles shouting: "Look at my hand. Look at my hand." The moderator called him to the front of the sanctuary and asked him to tell everyone what had happened. After he told us what had happened to his hand he asked: "Is it OK to say thank you, Jesus?" We of course gave him permission and he said: "Thank you! Jesus, Thank you! Jesus, Thank you Jesus." We later learned that he had never been in a Christian church before, but had studied under the Jehovah Witness. He is now a member of Boulder Street Church, has a job and is at the church whenever the doors are open.

This is an illustration of what the Revival is going to look like. There will be people simply walking into the churches and getting healed and saved.

He can change darkness to light
simply by His presence.

• • •

This was expressed in a vision by Korean Pastor Yon Wha Cho on September 22, 2010. It was translated into English, so I have printed it as given.

Word of God
> Joel 3:18-19 and Psalm 72:3
> 18 "In that day the mountains will drip new wine, and the hills will flow with milk; all the ravines of Judah will run with water. A fountain will flow out of the Lord's house and will water the valley of acacias"
> 19 "But Egypt will be desolate, Edom a desert waste, because of violence done to the people of Judah, in whose land they shed innocent blood."

Psalm 72:3 "The mountains will bring prosperity to the people, the hills the fruit of righteousness"

Vision

High mountain top and small mountain peaks surround a small basin, and the head of a dragon with horns rise up, but it's body like a huge centipede stretched out into many direction along the ridges and just looks like root of tree stretched down. At that moment a sound like thunder came from above saying "Look up" and saw the word written 'sword of Elijah' and the sword was descending and stopped above the head of dragon. Then a huge piece of hemp cloth being let down to earth by its four corners which remind me Act 10:11. Then my mind stirred by the voice ' I will renew this land as the valley of Hamonah where everything was purified ,cleansed and blessed that I will gladly received them' then I saw Jesus riding white horse which reminded me Revelation 19:11-16

I didn't understood this vision at that time but I understood it later while I prayed at Wednesday prayer meeting at Transform USA prayer center. The Lord spoke to me 'Tomorrow when you go to the Mt. Evans, do not do just sightseeing, but do prayer walk there' and that morning meeting I relayed this message to all to pray when they rise the mountain. In the car I prayed in tongue of confronting enemy until we reach the top of Evans. I missed to lead prayer all together there because of cold wind and too busy to take a picture of beauty around. When we start to descend, a lady came aside me and reminded me to pray at the mountain and I was ashamed and repented and when the car stopped on the way we all stand hand in hand over a cliff looking toward Denver city. We all cry out aloud in tongue. That place is called Mt Goliath and we could see many old trees fell over here and there. When we finished prayer the Lord said "Do you see those up-rooted trees? The force of Satan and Idols will be up-rooted like those through your prayer"

• • •

Letter from TC received on 11-19-2010

Dear Prayer Warrior:

I received this email from Mrs Cho, the Korean woman pastor who visited Colorado Springs a few weeks ago (early Oct) . She received the vision while staying at our center, which I shared with you a few weeks ago.

After she returned to Korea she happened to read the 'Revelation Glory' written by Ruth Ward Heflinin in the year 2000. She was also woman pastor and at that time active as a prophet like Cindy Jacob of today, but passed away a few years ago. Pastor Cho was surprised to find the exact same vision of hers in the book as follows:

Chapter 3 Seeing Things Happen Before They Happen

"I had a vision of the United States, and the focus was on the Rocky Mountains. I saw them coming down the country like a spine. I kept looking and kept seeing this great spine, a great backbone. I knew that what affected the spine would affect the entire country.

"I saw that the wealth of the Rockies from North to South had been mined and funneled into the rest of the country, and that now, instead of gold being mined from the Rockies, *God was going to rain down gold on the Rockies, on His people there, and that this would flow into the rest of the nation. I kept seeing golden rivers streaming forth from the mountains, spreading over the entire continent.*

"I also knew in that moment that there were regions of the Rocky Mountains that have never known a great move of God. Some of the western states don't have the same spiritual heritage as states that have been in existence longer. In those places where there was really no spiritual heritage from the past, I saw that God was going to give them their heritage in person, and from that great backbone, it would flow out to the rest of the country.'

"There was more to her vision. Much of the Rockies, she pointed out, was settled during the great Gold Rush days and many valuable minerals were mined in that area, enriching the nation. Now, she saw, God was about to send His golden glory over the Rocky Mountain area, and the resulting outpouring of the Holy Spirit would enrich the nation spiritually.

What a surprise! Praise the Lord!"

• • •

The following is an expression from a fellow believer written April 2, 2013, concerning the importance of the power of prayer and praise in revival:

"I saw a mountain with a river flowing down a mountain. And the mountain had seven levels and at each level the enemy, (an insidious red dragon) was coiled and ready for battle. At the first and highest level was the church in white robes and they were praying and searching themselves in repentance and singing praises to the Lord. And their prayers and praises were counted and weighed as the counting of an omer of fine and sifted flour. And they were receiving the blessings from the Lord like a river flowing through the top of the mountains and flowing downward. This was the first week of counting the omer. And the enemy was defeated through prayer and praise by the prayer and praises of the saints, and through the victory of the Lord as a sword danced about the head of the enemy, forcing it backward down the mountain.

"At the second level I saw family and friends ensnared by the dragon and trapped in it's coils. And the saints continued their trek down the mountain in prayer and praise. And their prayers and praises were counted and weighed as the counting of an omer of fine and sifted flour. And they were receiving the blessings from the Lord like a river flowing through the top of the mountains and flowing downward. This was the second week of counting the omer. And the enemy had to release his hold on family and friends to retreat from the oncoming and growing number of saints. And the sword of the Lord continued to dance near the head of the dragon, forcing it to continue its retreat down the mountain.

"At the third level of the mountain there was a plateau with a great many acquaintances who did not know the Lord and looked on in bewilderment. Some were offended and took up arms to arrest the movement of the saints while others began to rejoice at the joy of the Lord. The dragon tried with a grand sweep of its tail to remove those who would not join in his defense, but they joined in with the saints in praising the Lord and were provided white robes as they too began to pray and praise the Lord. And their prayers and praises were counted and weighed as the counting of an omer of fine and sifted flour. And they were receiving the blessings from the Lord like a river flowing through the top of the mountains and flowing downward. This was the third week of counting the omer. And the sword of the Lord and His saints continued to triumph over the dragon and forced it to retreat down the mountain.

"At the fourth level of the mountains were school buildings and students and teachers. And many of the teachers beheld the movement of the saints, and began to scheme to plant lies and deceptions in the path of the saints moving down the mountain. But the saints continued to sing their praises and pray to the Lord. And many of the teachers and students began to free the path of the saints through the schools of learning and knowledge, and began to declare the truth of the scriptures. These became saints themselves, and were given robes, and began to wind their way down the mountain with the other saints joining them in prayer and praises. And their prayers and praises were counted and weighed as the counting of an omer of fine and sifted flour. And they were receiving the blessings from the Lord like a river flowing through the top of the mountains and flowing downward. This was the fourth week of counting the omer. And with one dancing swoop, the sword of the Lord brushed aside the lies of the enemy, and continued forcing the dragon down the mountain.

"At the fifth level of the mountain were community businessmen and developers of industry. These were ensnared firmly by the dragon in its coils and the dragon guarded them jealously in its retreat. These the enemy held in a captivity of great fear. And many of these did not want to escape the coils of the dragon as they were afraid of destruction of their accumulated wealth, and did not trust the Lord to provide for them. Still, many others saw the peace of the Lord in the saints who sang praises as they prayed, and they released their fearful grip of the scales of the dragon and were set free. In so doing they found an abundance of provision and began to share their abundance with other saints in need. These were also given white robes and began to join the other saints on their way down the mountain. And their prayers and praises were counted and weighed as the counting of an omer of fine and sifted flour. And they were receiving the blessings from the Lord like a river flowing through the top of the mountains and flowing downward. This was the fifth week of counting the omer. And the dragon snarled and roared as it had no choice but to back away from the oncoming throng of saints and the sword of the Lord which danced ever closer to its head.

"At the sixth level of the mountain began rolling hills. And there were politicians and government leaders who were each certain that they knew the best course in which to lead others. And bevies of demons flew back and forth from the dragon to these leaders whispering words of arrogance and pride and puffing up the leaders. The dragon had no need to ensnare these with its coils as they were too large to move effectively and were hampered by their own egos and pride. Many of these began to try to persuade the saints to sing praise not only to the Lord, but to also sing to the dragon as they certainly could not persist forever in their downward march. These wanted appeasement. And attempted to lull the saints to sleep. Then, many other of the leaders sounded an alarm through unified voices in praise of the works and accomplishments of the Lord. These were given robes and joined the throng of saints continuing to march down the mountain. And their prayers and praises were counted and weighed as the counting of an omer of fine and sifted flour. And they were receiving the blessings from the Lord like a river flowing through the top of the mountains and flowing downward. This was the sixth week of counting the omer. And the enemy swiftly fled to the valley below the mountain in order to save itself and arrange a counter-strike at the oncoming saints and the sword of the Lord.

"At the seventh level of the mountain was a long slow slope leading to the valley where the enemy was ready to take its final stand. Here the saints rallied together as one body in the Lord. There were many differing nations' tribes and tongues who had been witnessing all the events that had occurred. Some were angry and fled the mountain to seek safety with the dragon. Many of these were killed by the dragon as they fled to it for safety. Many others on the seventh level of the mountain began to see clearly the course their lives had taken, and began to repent and pray to the Lord. And their prayers and praises were counted and weighed as the counting of an omer of fine and sifted flour. And they were receiving the blessings from the Lord like a river flowing through the top of the mountains and flowing downward. This was the seventh week of counting the omer. And the sword of the Lord went swiftly forward to subdue the dragon and its followers and they were dispersed much in the same way that the wind disperse smoke. And the blessings of the saints continued for its full season in accordance with the will of the Lord."

• • •

The springs begin in the mountains and the waters flow downhill. They soon become a trickle, then a stream, then a river, then a wider river that you cannot cross until it covers the whole land and flows into the oceans.

As we continue to pray we allow the Holy Spirit to work. The battle is His not ours. We need to pray and not faint.

• • •

A New York pastor said: "Many people are moving here to Colorado Springs from New York and New Jersey, so they can be here for the revival."

• • •

A visitor from Atlanta, Georgia came to the prayer meeting, as she was awakened at 3 a.m. in Georgia the Lord told her to study the Great Awakening of 1857-1858 because this coming revival will be comparable.

The Great Awakening was a layman's revival. Though ministers helped to counsel people, it was the lay people that carried it. At its peak there were an estimated 50,000 converts per week. During a two-year period, 10,000 were joining churches weekly, and Sunday schools flourished. The awakening brought over one million new converts into the American Church and revived the over four million members present before the revival.

• • •

We are called to prepare the land for the outpouring of the Holy Spirit. We are to spiritually clean house and rid the land of old ungodly inhabitants; take down the high places, rid the land of false gods, idols, and ungodly sacrifices.

• • •

Our weapons of choice are praise and worship as we claim this victory. We release the Spirit of God over this land and declare the outpouring of the Holy Spirit on our churches, pastors, teachers, musicians and declare that all who call upon the name of the Lord will be saved. We know that where the light shines, darkness has to flee. The light overcomes the darkness. We are also aware of the truth that where the light shines darkness is exposed. As the light shines on our churches, darkness will be exposed, and we are willing to deal with it as it comes. We declare that our churches will return to the Word of God and sound doctrine. We declare that all Christians will have a hunger for the Word of God and will seek truth. We declare that this land will become a haven and a sanctuary for people from all nations to come and receive healing and restoration due to the constant abiding of His presence.

—Prophecy given by David Bachoroski when we were praying in the Garden of the Gods.

As we continue to pray we allow the Holy Spirit to work. The battle is His not ours: prayer changes things. We need to pray and not faint, now is the time to get ready.

PRAY THE BLESSING

In the world today, there is One who hinders. He is keeping evil and sin at bay. Because of His presence evil is being restrained and cannot take over the world. Due to His presence the world is not destroyed. There is, however, a day coming soon when, "He who now restrains will do so until He is taken out of the way." 2nd Thessalonians 2:7 This restrainer, the one who hinders, is the Holy Spirit.

There remains a small window of opportunity until the Lord returns to take us home. He, (The Holy Spirit) who restrains will leave the earth with us, and that will be the end of the world as we know it. But until then, right now, "we wrestle not against flesh and blood but against principalities and powers in the heavenly places." Ephesians 6:12 When we begin calling flesh and blood the enemy we know that we are battling the wrong thing. We are among the ones who have been called by God to pray and intercede for this nation.

Romans 12:14 says that we are to "bless and curse not." This is the last time in the history of this world that we will have the privilege and honor of blessing those who persecute us and who speak all kinds of evil against us. I have heard Christians cursing the homosexual agenda, the abortionists, the President and certain political parties and agendas. We have not been called to curse. We have been called to bless.

"But I say to you who hear, love your enemies, do good to those who hate you, bless those who curse you. Pray for those who mistreat you. Whoever hits you on the cheek, offer him the other also; and whoever takes away your coat, do not withhold your shirt from him either. Give to everyone who asks of you, and whoever takes away what is yours, do not demand it back." Luke 6:27-30. Paul says: "Never pay back evil for evil to anyone. Respect what is right in the sight of all men. If possible, so far as it depends on you, be at peace with all men. Never take your own revenge, beloved, but leave room for the wrath of God, for it is written. 'Vengeance is Mine, I will repay, says the Lord.' But if your enemy is hungry, feed him, and if he is thirsty, give him a drink; for in so doing you will heap burning coals upon his head." (This destroys the enmity not the person). Do not be overcome by evil, but overcome evil with good." Romans 12:17-21 And further: "When we are reviled we bless, when we are persecuted, we endure." 1 Corinthians 4:12

In John 4:35 the Lord said; "Look on the fields; for they are white already to harvest," The crops are jumping up and down saying; "Pick Me! Pick Me!" "The harvest is plentiful, but the workers are few. Therefore, beseech the Lord of the harvest to send out workers into His harvest." Matthew 9:37-38 In the parable of the tares there was good seed sown; but while men were sleeping, his enemy came and sowed tares among the wheat, and went away. When the wheat sprang up and bore grain, then the tares became evident. And the slaves came to the master and said, 'did we not sow good seed in your field? How then does it have tares?' He said, 'An enemy has done this.' They asked him, 'Do you want us, then, to go and gather them up?' But he said, 'No lest while you are gathering up the tares, you may root up the wheat with them. Allow both to grow together until the harvest.' Matthew 13:25-30 paraphrased. The more we try to pull up the tares, the more we damage the wheat. Don't hurt the wheat. The Lord said He would take care of the tares.

Say you're in your car and stopped at a red light, you see a blind person ahead of you in the crosswalk with a white cane, tapping the road to get across. When the light turns green you patiently wait for him to cross. You don't honk your horn and yell at him to hurry up. You bless him with your patience and allow him to cross the road at his own pace. Ten cars back a person is honking his horn because he doesn't know what's going on. This is how it is with many in the church who are not patient with the blind and unbelieving. They don't understand what's going on and want to curse the blind man instead of leading him to the light.

In the same way Satan has blinded the eyes of the unbelieving, they need you to bless them and pray for them that they will find their way. "And even if our gospel is veiled, it is veiled to those who are perishing, in whose case the god of the world has blinded the minds of the unbelieving, that they might not see the light of the gospel of the Glory of Christ, who is the image of God." 2 Corinthians 4:3-4 "He delivered us from the domain of darkness, and transferred us to the kingdom of His beloved Son." Colossians 1:13

The greatest blessing you can give a person, an organization, or the government, is the blessing of the presence of God coming into their lives. He can change darkness to light simply by His presence.

Nowhere in the Epistles did Paul ever rail a judgment or a curse against the Roman government, although it was one of the most ungodly governments in its day. They burned Christians as candles in the coliseums; they used lions to attack Christians for entertainment. Paul said to pray for those who are in authority. Don't pray a curse; pray a blessing. As the nation is blessed you are blessed. When you walk into a dark room you don't need to curse the darkness, turn on the light. We are called to be a light in a dark place, walk as children of the light.

PROTECTED IN GLORY!

After the Lord called me out of darkness into His marvelous light in 1972. I went for a period of three days without any sleep. I was afraid that if I did not hold on to Him, He would leave me, and I would be in the darkness once again. I thought

153

that it was up to me to hang onto Him, instead of me trusting Him to hang on to me. After becoming totally exhausted I came to the end of myself. I knew I had to take a chance and trust Him. I laid down on the couch and prayed. "Lord I'm going to sleep and get the rest I need. I'm trusting you to protect me and if you are gone when I wake up, so be it. I've done all I can do." What I discovered when I woke up about an hour later was that He was still there. I later learned that the passage: "I will never leave you nor forsake you," Hebrews 13:5 was true. I was beginning to trust Him.

"As you therefore have received Christ Jesus the Lord (redemption), so walk in Him (regeneration)." Colossians 2:6 The first question comes to mind. How did you receive Christ Jesus the Lord? The answer of course is; by grace through faith. "For by grace you have been saved through faith; and not of yourselves, it is a gift of God;" Ephesians 2:8. This is called redemption.

The second question is: How do you walk in Him? The answer is the same as the first; by grace through faith! "For it is God who is at work in you, both to will and to work for His good pleasure." Philippians 2:13. This is called regeneration.

Let's settle this thing once and for all. "We, who are *protected by the power of God* through faith for a salvation ready to be revealed in the last time." 1 Peter 1:5. "The Lord is faithful, and He will strengthen and protect you from the evil one." 2 Thessalonians 3:3 Is this true or false? Of course, it's true.

In these last days there will be two classes of born-again Christians: those who try to protect themselves, and those who trust the Lord to protect them. In both cases they are redeemed and will go to heaven when they die. The first group will struggle and battle through life to try to protect themselves. The second group will rest in the arms of Jesus and trust Him to battle for them and protect them. Which group are you in? I have found that there are times when I am so worried about myself that I don't have time for others. There are those Christians who spend so much time battling the enemy that they don't have time for God. It is very difficult to have concern for others when we are worried about ourselves. It's not about you! *This life in Christ is all about Him.*

Believe the Love! "And we have come to know and have *believed the love* which God has for us." 1 John 4:16 "For I know whom I have believed and I am convinced that He is able to guard what I have entrusted to Him until that day." 2 Timothy 1:12

In the year of the reformation, in 1529 Martin Luther wrote the following great hymn:

A Mighty Fortress Is Our God

A mighty Fortress is our God, a trusty shield and
  weapon;
He helps us free from every need that hath us now
  o'ertaken.
The old evil foe, Now means deadly woe;
Deep guile and great might, Are his dread arms in fight;
On earth is not his equal.

With might of ours can naught be done, Soon were our
  loss effected;
But for us fights the Valiant One, Whom God Himself
  elected,
Ask ye, Who that may be? Jesus Christ it is He.
Of Sabbath Lord, And there is none other God;
He holds the field forever.

Tho' devils all the world should fill, All eager to devour
  us,
We tremble not, we fear no ill, They shall not overpower
  us,
This world's prince may still, scowl fierce as he will,
He can harm us none, He's judged; the deed is done;
One little word can fell him.

The Word they still shall let remain, Nor any thanks
   have for it;
He's by our side upon the plain, With His good gifts
   and Spirit.
And take they our life, Goods, fame, child, and wife,
Let these all be gone, They yet have nothing won;
The Kingdom ours remaineth.

Oh Lord, forgive me for being so foolish as to think, that I need to protect myself. Lord, You are my protection, You are my strength, You are the one who keeps my foot from being caught in the snare of the trapper. I pray that you will give me the Grace to trust You. You are my provider, deliverer and my strength. Thank you for allowing me to trust You. Thank you for giving me the Grace to believe the Love that You have for me.

Speaking of protection, have you ever noticed there are those Christians who believe they need to protect God. God doesn't need your protection. He needs your obedience.

Elisha came near to all the people and said, "How long *will* you hesitate between two opinions? If the LORD is God, follow Him; but if Baal, follow him." But the people did not answer him a word...And he said, "Fill four pitchers with water and pour *it* on the burnt offering and on the wood." And he said, "Do it a second time," and they did it a second time. And he said, "Do it a third time," and they did it a third time. The water flowed around the altar and he also filled the trench with water. Then the fire of the LORD fell and consumed the burnt offering and the wood and the stones and the dust, and licked up the water that was in the trench. When all the people saw it, they fell on their faces; and they said, "The LORD, He is God; the LORD, He is God." 1 Kings 21-39 excerpts. Did you notice that Elisha did not need to protect God, God told him what to do and he did it, no excuses, no alibis — *he just obeyed.*

Jesus did not try to protect the Father when he asked Peter to come to Him on the water. He knew the wind was coming up, and everyone knows that it is much easier to walk on water on a calm day rather than on a windy day. God told Him what to do and He did it, no excuses, no alibis, he just obeyed the Father.

When Jesus was asked to heal Lazarus, He was obedient to the Father and waited another three days. When He got there, Lazarus was already dead three days. Didn't He know that it is much easier to raise a person from the dead after two days rather than waiting for three days? God told Him what to do and He did it, no excuses, no alibis. He just obeyed the Father.

In this revival that is taking over the nation, Christians need to be obedient as we allow the presence of God to work in and through us. Sometimes we are scared to obey because of fear. What if God doesn't act? I will look stupid, so what. We also don't need to use parlor tricks, deception, lies or showbiz in our obedience. We are to be people of integrity and obedience.

Do you realize: "From everyone who has been given much, much will be required; and to whom they entrusted much, of him they will ask all the more." Luke 12:48 Years ago I was praying, and complaining, about a certain task that the Lord was asking me to do and He said to me; "He to whom much is given, much is required." And I said; "Yes Lord, but to him to whom much is required, of You much is expected." If He is requiring obedience from you, you can expect His provision.

When darkness surrounds us…when our enemies arise…whom shall we fear? You alone Lord are our light and our salvation. How shall we then be moved? Will You not great Father of Glory rise up on our behalf? Will You not, as in days of old cause Your voice to be heard? Will You not show the lightning down Your arm? Will You not with indignation and anger...with the flame of a devouring fire...scatter our enemies? We will call upon You trusting...not in our own merits Lord, but in the merits...in the authority of our love-scarred Redeemer. Of whom then shall we be afraid? (Prayer by John Hayes)

The Glory of Man
Section Five

Glory In Persecution

GLORY IN PERSECUTION

There is a large part of the Body of Christ that is dormant because of persecution. If this dormant church can be revitalized and brought back into the fold, we would truly have a church triumphant.

In Mark 4:16-17, The Lord explains the parable of the seed sown on stony ground. The Amplified Bible says: "And in the same way the ones sown upon stony ground are those who, when they hear the Word, at once receive and accept and welcome it with joy; And they have no real root in themselves, and so they endure for a little while, then when trouble or persecution arises on account of the Word, they immediately are offended - become displeased, indignant, resentful; and they stumble and fall away."

We all know people in our own circle of friends who have become 'offended, displeased, indignant and resentful' because of the Word, or their understanding of the Word.

Webster's defines persecution: "To cause to suffer because of belief." I say that, "persecution is something that is done in the physical, spiritual, emotional or mental realms to make you doubt God's Love." We often think of persecution as a missionary put in jail or beaten because of preaching the Gospel. I have never seen a missionary return home after persecution and say, "I Quit." However, I have seen those who have no real root in themselves fall away because of the type of persecution that causes them to become 'offended, displeased, indignant and resentful.'

In his book, *The Heavenly Man*, Liu Zhenying, affectionately known as Christian Brother Yun says: "In China I had been used to beatings, torture with electric batons, and all kinds of humiliation. I guess that deep in my heart I had presumed that now that I was in the West my days of persecution had ended. In China, Christians are persecuted with beatings and imprisonment. In the West, Christians are persecuted by the words of other Christians." "This new kind of spiritual persecution was no easier than physical persecution in China, just different."

Brother Yun continues: "The people who really suffer are those who never experience God's presence. The way to have God's presence is by walking through hardship and suffering — the way of the cross. You may not be beaten or imprisoned for your faith, but I am convinced each Christian will still have a cross to bear in his or her life. In the West it may be ridicule, slander, or rejection. When you're faced with such trials, the key is not to run from them or fight them, but to embrace them as friends. When you do this you'll not fail to experience God's presence and help." [1]

WHO WILL BE PERSECUTED?

"All who desire to live godly in Christ Jesus will be persecuted." 2 Timothy 3:12

Every Christian who desires to live godly in Christ Jesus will be persecuted. This is not an option. It will happen. We should not be surprised when it comes. Situations will occur that can cause us to become 'offended, displeased, indignant and resentful.' This will most often occur in the Body of Christ where our expectations are the highest. We are not usually surprised when persecuted by the world because we expect it and they have met our expectations. *"What are these wounds between your arms? Then he will say, 'Those with which I was wounded in the house of my Friends.'"* Zechariah 13:6 The Lord was wounded in the house of His friends. Can you expect it to be different with you? When we are hurt or persecuted by the Body of Christ, it hurts the most because we do not expect it. Our expectations are that these are holy people and we expect more from them. If the enemy could not stop you from becoming a Christian he will do everything possible to cause you to become 'offended, displeased, indignant or resentful.' By doing this he will remove your effectiveness in the Body of Christ.

In Matthew 10:16-28 The Lord teaches about persecution. Then in verse 29-31 He says: "Are not two sparrows sold for a cent? And yet not one of them will fall to the ground apart from your Father. But the very hairs of your head are all numbered. Therefore do not fear; you are of more value than many sparrows."

There are two classes of Christians who will be persecuted. (1) Me and, (2) All other Christians. The hairs of your head represents Me. All other Christians are represented by the sparrows. We need to expect that our children, parents, friends and all other Christians will be persecuted.

We have all heard a parent say: "I don't care what you do to me, just don't hurt my kids, (parents or siblings)." Many times it is much easier to take the persecution ourselves than to see our kids get hurt. We need to trust the Lord when He says He will protect the sparrows.

> "...but whoever causes one of these little ones who believe in Me to stumble, it is better for him that a heavy millstone be hung around his neck, and that he be drowned in the depth of the sea." Matthew 18:6

FEAR

In Matthew 10:26,28 and 31 The Lord, while speaking about persecutions, repeatedly says *"Do not Fear."* When we or our loved ones are persecuted and we respond by becoming 'offended, displeased, indignant or resentful', it is usually due to fear. Not trusting the Lord to defend, protect and save you or your loved ones.

Faith is trust in God. Fear is trust in evil.

Satan will do everything he can to keep fear involved in our lives. He will do everything he can to make us doubt God's love for us. Fear is the only way he has of getting a foothold in our lives. It is the connector to darkness.

"Perfect love casts out all fear." 1 John 4:18 We need to understand and believe (trust in, and totally rely on) the love God has for us.

The love that God has for us is based on His covenant with the Son. The New Covenant is based on the shed blood of Jesus Christ. It is an eternal covenant, therefore it cannot be changed or broken.

> "Who shall separate us from the love of Christ? Shall tribulation, or distress, or persecution, or famine, or nakedness, or peril, or sword? ...But in all these things we overwhelmingly conquer through Him who loved us." Romans 8:35- 37

> "For I am convinced that neither death, nor life, nor angels, nor principalities, nor things present, nor things to come, nor powers, nor height, nor depth, nor any other created thing, shall be able to separate us from the love of God, which is in Christ Jesus our Lord." Romans 8:38-39

> "...in order that in Christ Jesus the blessing of Abraham might come to the Gentiles, (us) so that we might receive the promise of the Spirit through faith." Galatians 3:14 The blessings of Abraham are found in Deuteronomy 28:2-14.

> *When suffering comes as it must, remind me Lord that our Savior suffered on my behalf for Your Glory. How can I think it unlikely that You might privilege me to suffer for His glory? We remember Paul and Silas singing Your praises in chains and how the Philippian jailer and his family were changed forever. Your Word says that we are to rejoice in the Lord*

always, love to sing Your praises, and thank You when good things happen, but hardship also happens. How quick am I to sing Your praises and thank You in such times. Bad times have come — they surely shall come again. Protect me in the future from considering ways of escape... Teach me to consider and seek only Your Glory. (Prayer by John Hayes)

PERSECUTION ON TWO FRONTS

A. What to do if you are persecuted.

B. How to lead others back who have been persecuted.

What to do if you are persecuted.

When we are in His will, we are in the safest place in the world.

"If a man's ways are pleasing to the Lord, He makes even his enemies to be at peace with him."
Proverbs 16:7

First look to yourself. Is there something I'm doing to antagonize or cause a person to become offended, displeased, indignant and resentful?

"Beloved, do not be surprised at the fiery ordeal among you, which comes upon you for your testing, as though some strange thing were happening to you; but to the degree that you share the sufferings of Christ, keep on rejoicing; so that also at the revelation of His glory, you may rejoice with exultation. If you are reviled for the name of Christ, you are blessed, because the Spirit of glory and of God rests upon you." 1 Peter 4:12-14

Love does not take into account a wrong suffered.
1 Corinthians 13:5 (paraphrased)

165

As a Christian we are to be led by the Word of God and the Holy Spirit. We are not to be led by the actions or reactions of those who would seek to make us to become offended, displeased, indignant or resentful. When we allow ourselves to be led by the actions or reactions of others we are not being led by the Holy Spirit.

"I will say of the Lord, He is my refuge and my fortress, my God, on Him I lean and rely, and in him I (confidently) trust." Psalm 91:2 Amplified Bible

"For He will give His angels (especial) charge over you, to accompany and defend and preserve you in all your ways." Psalm 91:11 Amplified Bible

"Whenever they persecute you in this city flee to the next." Matthew 10:23

"But I say to you, love your enemies, and pray for those who persecute you." Matthew 5:44

"Blessed are those who have been persecuted for the sake of righteousness, for theirs is the kingdom of heaven. Blessed are you when men revile you, and persecute you, and say all kinds of evil against you falsely, on account of Me. Rejoice, and be glad, for your reward in heaven is great, for so they persecuted the prophets who were before you." Matthew 5:10-12

"Let all bitterness and wrath and anger and clamor and slander be put away from you, along with all malice. And be kind to one another, tender-hearted, forgiving each other, just as God in Christ also has forgiven you." Ephesians 4:31-32

How to lead others back who have been persecuted.

"For the Son of Man has come to save that which was lost. What do you think? If any man has a hundred sheep, and one of them has gone astray, does he not leave the ninety-nine on the mountains and go and search for the one that is straying? And if it turns out that he find it, truly I say to you, he rejoices over it more than over the ninety-nine which have not gone astray." Matthew 18:11-13

Go seek the one who has strayed. The kindness of God will lead him back, not our condemnation or accusations.

"Or do you think lightly of the riches of His kindness and forbearance and patience, not knowing that the kindness of God leads you to repentance?" Romans 2:4

"And we urge you, brethren, admonish the unruly, encourage the fainthearted, help the weak, be patient with all men." 1 Thessalonians 5:14

"Encourage the exhausted, and strengthen the feeble. Say to those with palpitating heart, take courage, fear not. Behold, your God will come with vengeance; the recompense of God will come, but He will save you." Isaiah 35:3-4

"And yet do not regard him as an enemy, but admonish him as a brother." 2 Thessalonians 3:15

We are to pray for them with intercessory prayer. Do you realize that God is a gentleman and will not force His way into anybody's life, but He will go where He is invited? The person who is hurt may not invite Him into their lives, but we can give the Lord an invitation to go to that person and ask Him to make them whole and restore them to the Body of Christ. We know that the Lord will act when we pray and will give them an opportunity to be restored.

"...Yet He Himself bore the sin of many, and interceded for the transgressors." Isaiah 53:12

"Therefore He is able to save forever those who draw near to God through Him, since He always lives to make intercession for them." Hebrews 7:25

We are to stand for those who cannot stand, weep with those who have no more tears, pray for those who have no more desire to pray.

PERSECUTION BY THE ENEMY

There are three sources of persecution, things that make you to become 'offended, displeased, indignant or resentful:' The devil, the world and our own flesh.

The Devil

I have heard it said that, "We do not have persecution in the United States." One trick of the enemy is to get you to believe that it doesn't exist. If you believe something does not exist, you will not battle it.

The enemy will do everything he can to get you to doubt God's love. This is done either by physical, spiritual, emotional or mental persecution.

"The thief comes only to steal, and kill, and destroy; I came that they might have life, and might have it abundantly." John 10:10

"For though we walk in the flesh, we do not war according to the flesh, for the weapons of our warfare are not of the flesh, but divinely powerful for the destruction of fortresses. We are destroying speculations and every lofty thing raised up against the knowledge of God, and we are taking every thought captive to the obedience of Christ." 2 Corinthians 10:3-5

"...In this you greatly rejoice, even though now for a little while, *if necessary*, you have been distressed by various trials, ..." 1 Peter 1:6

The World

Condemnation takes you to Sinai. Conviction takes you to Calvary. The word given on Mount Sinai can only condemn us of our sin, it gives no power to keep it. The WORD spoken at Calvary will convict of our sin but will also pay the penalty for our sin and gives us the power to walk in His holiness.

"These things I have spoken to you that you may be kept from stumbling. They will make you outcasts from the synagogue; but an hour is coming for everyone who kills you to think that he is offering service to God. And these things they will do, because they have not known the Father, or Me." John 16:1-3

Our Flesh

"But we have this treasure in earthen vessels, that the surpassing greatness of the power may be of God and not from ourselves; we are afflicted in every way, but not crushed; perplexed, but not despairing; persecuted, but not forsaken; struck down, but not destroyed; always carrying about in the body the dying of Jesus, that the life of Jesus also may be manifested in our body." 2 Corinthians 4:7-11

"...he who was born according to the flesh persecuted him who was born according to the Spirit, so it is now also." Galatians 4:29

Sometimes persecution may come as a result of our own disobedience. Persecution does not mean you are out of the will of God. A lack of persecution does not mean you are in the will of God.

We have a job to do given to us by the Lord. We must not

become distracted by persecution and allow it to take our eyes off our mission. As a Christian we are responsible *to* others, we are not responsible *for* others. That is the Lord's job.

"And Jesus came up and spoke to them saying. "All authority has been given to Me in heaven and on earth. Go therefore and make disciples of all the nations, baptizing them in the name of the Father and the Son and the Holy Spirit, teaching them to observe all that I commanded you; and lo, I am with you always, even to the end of the age." Matthew 28:18-20

PUBLICANS AND SINNERS

We are to be available to go wherever the Lord leads us to speak to those who have strayed.

"And it happened that as He was reclining at table in the house, behold many tax-gathers and sinners came and joined Jesus and His disciples at the table. And when the Pharisees saw this, they said to His disciples. "Why does your Teacher eat with the tax-gatherers and sinners?" But when He heard this, He said, "It is not those who are healthy who need a physician, but those who are ill, but go and learn what this means, 'I desire compassion and not sacrifice,' for I did not come to call the righteous, but sinners." Matthew 9:10-13

"But to what shall I compare this generation? It is like children sitting in the market places, who call out to the other children, and say, 'We played the flute for you, and you did not dance; we sang a dirge, and you did not mourn.' For John came neither eating nor drinking, and they say, He has a demon!' The Son of Man came eating and drinking, and they say, 'Behold, a gluttonous man and a drunkard, a friend of tax-gatherers and sinners!' Yet wisdom is vindicated by her deeds." Matthew 11:16-19

"Now all the tax-gatherers and the sinners were coming near Him to listen to Him. And both the Pharisees and the scribes began to grumble, saying, 'This man receives sinners and eats with them.'" Luke 15:1-2

In your quest to win your lost brother do not be afraid of what others might say. This job is more important than that.

"And after that He went out, and noticed a tax-gatherer named Levi, sitting in the tax office, and He said to him, "Follow Me." And Levi gave a big reception for Him in his house; and there was a great crowd of tax-gatherers and other people who were reclining at table with them. And the Pharisees and their scribes began grumbling at His disciples, saying, "Why do you eat and drink with the tax-gatherers and sinners?" And Jesus answered and said to them, "It is not those who are well who need a physician, but those who are sick. I have not come to call righteous men, but sinners to repentance." Luke 5:27-32

"But if your brother sins, go and show him his fault in private; if he listens to you, you have won your brother. But if he does not listen to you, take one or two more with you, so that by the mouth of two or three witnesses every fact may be confirmed. If he refuses to listen to them, tell it to the church; and if he refuses to listen even to the church, let him be to you as a Gentile and a tax collector." Matthew 18:15-17

Notice how the Lord treated tax-gatherers and sinners. He ate with them and did everything possible to bring them into the kingdom.

"Now we command you, brethren, in the name of our Lord Jesus Christ that you keep away from every brother who leads an unruly life and not according to the tradition which you received from us." 2 Thessalonians 3:6

"And yet do not regard him as an enemy, but admonish him as a brother." 2 Thessalonians 3:15

COME HOME

If we, in the church, have done anything to cause you to become 'offended, displeased, indignant or resentful', I apologize. If you have been hurt by other believers or the church I urge you to come home. If you cannot return to your own church I urge you to find a church home where you can be used of the Lord. The Lord urges us to forgive one another as God for Christ sake also has forgiven you. The Amplified Bible puts it this way:

"Let all bitterness and indignation and wrath (passion, rage, bad temper) and resentment (anger, animosity) and quarreling, (brawling, clamor, contention) and slander (evil speaking, abusive or blasphemous language) be banished from you, with all malice (spite, ill will or baseness of any kind). And become useful and helpful and kind to one another, tenderhearted (compassionate, understanding, loving-hearted), forgiving one another (readily and freely), as God in Christ forgave you." Ephesians 4:31-32 Amplified Bible

Do you realize that, "if one member suffers, all the members suffer with it" 1 Corinthians 12:26 "But now there are many members, but one body. And the eye cannot say to the hand, "I have no need of you." or again the head to the feet. "I have no need of you." On the contrary, it is much truer that the members of the body which seem to be weaker are necessary." 1 Corinthians 12:20-22

The church needs every part of the body operating in an effective manner to become strong. I need to hear what the Lord has taught you, and you need to hear what the Lord has taught me. One lone stick can be broken quite easily, but a group of sticks are much stronger and cannot be broken because they are joined together. If you, my brother, are alone you can be broken and hurt quite easily. I urge you to come and join with the body and be strengthened.

In an orchestra all the members need to be playing together in order to make beautiful music. If one member is out playing by himself, he may be playing very well, but is not making beautiful music because he only plays a small part of the whole. He needs the other parts joining with him to be effective.

"Let us consider how to stimulate one another to love and good deeds, not forsaking our own assembling together, as is the habit of some, but encouraging one another; and all the more, as you see the day drawing near." Hebrews 10:24,25

GLORY IN TESTING

The following are some of the truths concerning Biblical testing that I have learned through over 30 years of testing cars for the General Motors Proving Grounds.

First let's start with a basic definition of testing according to Webster:

To Test
1. An examination or trial, as of something's value.
2. An event that tries one's qualities, testing the worth and character.
3. A set of questions, problems, etc. for determining one's knowledge, abilities etc.

To Prove

1. To test by experiment or standard.
2. To establish as true — to be found by experiment or trial.

Now let's look at the Biblical definition according to Strong's Concordance:

Temptation

1. Peirazo (Greek) — To test, endeavor, scrutinize, entice, discipline, examine, prove, tempt. Matthew 4:1, 1 Corinthians 10:13
2. Peirasmos (Greek) — Putting to proof, by experiment, Temptation. James 1:2, 2 Peter 2:9

Try

1. Dokimazo (Greek) — To test, allow, discern, examine. 1 Corinthians 3:13
2. Dokimion (Greek) — A testing, trustworthiness, test, experience, proof, trial. James 1:3

The following is a true story to illustrate one truth about testing:

Careening down the mountain, smoke pouring out of the wheel wells, the sickening odor of burning brake pads filling your nostrils with a stench that can last for days. Your observer tells you that you're at a thousand degrees and the temperatures are rising. You're coming to the most hazardous part of the course—hairpin turns. Keep your wits about you, don't let your mind wander, rely on the gauges and your experience. Watch the....

Testing — The very thought of the word can cause a tightness in the pit of your stomach. It can cause sweaty palms and your pulse rate to rise. The following are some of the truths concerning testing that I have learned through over 30 years of testing cars for the General Motors Proving Ground on Pikes Peak.

We put the vehicles' components through an examination or trial to test its value. This is done to establish as true the components worth or character or to prove it. A test is an event that tries one's qualities. When the Lord gives you a quality such as faith, love, joy, peace, patience, goodness, i.e. the Fruit of the Spirit as in Galatians 5:22, He then proves that quality to establish it as true by experience or trial in your life.

A *test* is to prove to you what you have, not to prove it to others. A *trial* is to prove to others what has been given to you.

The Lord will never test in your life what you do not have. We do not run a tire test with a spark plug; we run a tire test with a known good tire to prove or establish as true the value of that tire. God will only test what we have been given, not what we don't have. That is why when you pray for patience, the proof that you have that patience you prayed for is the test that follows. This proves to you that the Lord has heard your prayer and has enacted that quality in you.

When you received Jesus into your life you were given the Fruit of the Spirit. But they were not made real to you until you accepted them as part of your new life in Christ, and God proved to you that you have those qualities. He proved it, or established it as true, in your daily experience by trials or tests.

I do not test cars because I hate cars, but instead it is because I love cars and want to make them better. God does not put us to the test because He hates us and wants to punish us, (Christ took our punishment for us), but instead because He loves us and wants us to live a victorious life by knowing what He has given us in Christ Jesus.

I hit the brake pedal for the last time. There was nothing left. I found the breaking point. I knew what we had to do to make the car better. We were coming to one of the hottest parts of the course with nothing left…

We test cars beyond the breaking point of everyday usage. Every part is tested to the extreme of operating conditions. A word of encouragement to you—God is faithful. 1 Corinthians 10:13 says, "No temptation has overtaken you, but such as is common to man; and God is faithful who will not allow you to be tempted beyond what you are able, but with the temptation will provide the way of escape. Also, that you may be able to endure it." God knows your breaking point and will not allow you to be tested beyond it. He knows just what He's doing; He created you and knows all about you. Testing is designed to build you up, not to tear you down.

Now we can better understand James 1:2-4 where He says, "Consider it all joy, my brethren, when you encounter various trials, knowing that the testing of your faith produces endurance. And let endurance have its perfect result, that you may be perfect and complete, lacking in nothing." And James 1:12 says, "Blessed is a man who perseveres under trial; for once he has been approved, (passed the test) he will receive the Crown of Life, which the Lord has promised to those who love Him."

There was only one thing to do. Let the brakes cool. They would re-cover if I could only let them cool. I must stop the car… I dropped the transmission into low gear; there was some slowing, but not enough. The hill was getting steeper. I must stop the car… Finally, "the way of escape": I came to a wide spot in the road and powered to a 180-degree spin. We were now going back up the hill, the brakes would now cool as it coasted to a stop.

"You, who are protected by the power of God through faith for a salvation ready to be revealed in the last time. In this you greatly rejoice, even though now for a little while, if necessary, you have been distressed by various trials, so that the proof of your faith, being more precious than gold which is perishable, even though tested by fire, may be found to result in praise and glory and honor at the revelation of Jesus Christ;" 1 Peter 1:4-7

I believe that the highest kind of praise that we can give to God is to *trust Him* when we are going through various tests and trials.

2 Corinthians 9:8 says "And God is able to make all grace abound to you, that always having all sufficiency in everything, you may have an abundance for every good deed."

So, as you can see a test is an event that tries one's qualities to prove or establish as true by experience or trial. The Lord is merely showing to you what He has already given you in Christ Jesus. Praise God for His willingness to share His life with us!

My observer was calmly taking the last of the test data and finishing his report. "He trusted me." He smiled as I looked at him and said, "Thank You."

The Glory of Man
Section Six

Our National Glory

OUR NATIONAL GLORY

Our country was founded by a group of Christians called Puritans who came to escape the religious persecution they experienced in England. "Puritanism was the result of measuring the conduct of public officials by scriptural standards." [1]

The Puritans were strong supporters of the "separation of Church and State." The name puritan was a derogatory name, hoisted upon them by the Queen of England. It referred to those who refused to bow to the liturgy, ceremonies and discipline of the church. The state church was under government control, and the government dictated to the church what it needed to teach. This was known as the Church of England or the Anglican Church.

Yet the public acknowledgement of God was more than just a pleasant practice in early America; it actually formed the basis of our government philosophy — a philosophy set forth in eighty-four simple words in the *Declaration of Independence*.

"We hold these truths to be self-evident: that all men are created equal, that they are endowed by their Creator with certain unalienable rights; that among these are life, liberty and the pursuit of happiness. To secure these rights, governments are instituted among men, deriving their just powers from the consent of the governed. That whenever any form of government becomes destructive of these ends, it is the right of the people to alter or to abolish it, and to institute new government, laying its foundation on such principles and organizing its powers in such form, as to them shall seem most likely to effect their safety and happiness."

Unalienable, is another word for eternal—not subject to change under any circumstances. It implies that there are moral absolutes.

Thus, five immutable principles constitute the heart and soul of American government:

1. Government acknowledges that there is a Creator.
2. Government acknowledges that the Creator gives specific unalienable rights to man.
3. Government acknowledges that it exists to protect God-given rights.
4. Government acknowledges that below the level of God-given rights, government powers are to be operated only with the permission of citizens — i.e., with the "consent of the governed."
5. If government fails to meet the four standards above, the people have an unalienable right to abolish that government and institute a new one that does observe the four criteria above." [2] Excerpts from WallBuilders. com

"Significantly, without a public and official recognition of God, there is no hope of limited government, for rights come only from God or from man. If rights come from God, then we can require man to protect those rights — as we did in the *Declaration of Independence*, *Constitution*, and *Bill of Rights*. But if our rights come from man, then man is permitted to regulate or abolish those rights, and government's power over our lives therefore becomes absolute and unlimited, as has been the growing trend since the 1990s."

"The Founders understood that irrevocable limitations can be placed on government *only* when God is recognized as the source of our rights; they also understood that if we became complacent in our recognition of God as the center of our lives and government, then we would lose our liberties, as Thomas Jefferson warned."

"According to Jefferson, the only *firm basis* of our national liberties is a *conviction in the minds of the people* that our liberties are from God and that government cannot intrude into those liberties without incurring God's wrath." [2] Excerpts from WallBuilders.com

"George Washington knew well that a nation's laws spring from its morals and that its morals spring from its religion. And the religion of which Washington spoke was clear to all who knew him: "It is impossible to govern rightly without God and the Bible." [3] Benjamin Hart

"Because that which is known about God is evident within them; for God made it evident to them. For since the creation of the world His invisible attributes, His eternal power and divine nature, have been clearly seen, being understood through what has been made, so that they are without excuse." Romans.1:19-20.

With no higher lawgiver, the state becomes the highest moral authority, in which case rights are no longer "unalienable," but become subject to the whim of the monarch, dictator, assembly, or the vicissitudes of human fashion. Therefore, Paul warns in his letter to the Romans:

"Let every person be in subjection to the governing authorities. For there is no authority except from God." Romans 13:1

"The underlying current in our country has always been the Bible and Christianity. The morality has been anchored in God's Word. Supreme Court Justice John Marshall said that the government of the United States is a "government of laws and not men." If there is no consensus as to what constitutes the law, often called the "Higher Law," and where it can be found, then we are governed by men and not laws. The colonists believed that this "Higher Law" was a definite thing and could be found in the Bible. The notion of the "Higher Law" goes all the way back to Moses, when God handed down His commandments to the people of Israel for their protection. God through Moses taught the Israelites how to live with each other, how to order their moral lives and their community and how to please Him.

In 1980 the Supreme Court ruled that Kentucky's decision to post the Ten Commandments in the public schools was a violation of the First Amendment's clause forbidding the establishment of religion. Thus, for public schools to teach the true origin of America's common law heritage, which undergirds the U.S. Constitution, and which is specifically referred to in the Seventh Amendment, is now deemed "unconstitutional." This ruling followed the equally astounding decision in 1962 and 1963 banning all religious expression from the public schools. James Madison and Fisher Ames had in mind when they introduced the First Amendment, which was intended to guarantee "the free exercise" of religion, not "obliterate" religion." [3] Benjamin Hart

"For though we walk in the flesh, we do not war according to the flesh, for the weapons of our warfare are not of the flesh, but divinely powerful for the destruction of fortresses. We are destroying speculations and every lofty thing raised up against the knowledge of God, and we are taking every thought captive to the obedience of Christ." 2 Corinthians 10:3-5.

"To grant us that we, being delivered from the hand of our enemies. Might serve Him without fear, in

holiness and righteousness before Him all our days."
Luke 1:74-75

"If My people who are called by My name humble
themselves and pray and seek My face and turn from their
wicked ways, then I will hear from heaven, will forgive
their sin and will heal their land." 2 Chronicles 7:14.

The above passage isn't calling everybody to do this, only
those who are called by His name. Can you imagine if those
politicians, educators and those in any position of authority who
dare to call themselves Christians would humble themselves and
pray and seek His face, what would happen in our nation? Do
you think this could have any impact on changing our nation
back to God? Can you imagine what our country would be
like if we measured the conduct of public officials by scriptural
standards? What about our own lives?

"Surely His salvation is near to those who fear Him
that glory may dwell in our land." Psalm 85:9-13

*We lift up our national, state, county, and city
leaders. Protect us from the worldly and foolish among
them. Many such would be swift to hinder Christian
testimonies, witnessing, and the furthering of Your
Kingdom. Unless such limitations serve your purposes,
Lord Stymie their devices...thwart their treachery. We
thank You that except You allowed it none could have
risen to power for they are in positions to seriously
influence our lives for good or evil. We're grateful that
our dependence is on You not on them, and that You
turn the heart of the king any way You want. Turn
them O God, from darkness to light, from Satan to
Christ, and from death to life. Let our nation continue
to send laborers to the lost both at home and abroad.
Send many witnesses to those unsaved leaders who
will listen.*

O Lord we thank You for godly men and women in leadership. Undergird, strengthen, encourage and bless each leader worldwide. Pour Your Spirit out upon them and the fear of God into them. Guide their decisions Lord, Protect them from their enemies and Yours. Give them Your wisdom, prudence, and understanding. May they season the halls of government with salt and brighten them with light. (Prayers by John Hayes)

EGYPT TO CANAAN

It is kind of hard to remember the original intent was to drain the swamp, when you're up to your armpits in alligators.

"He brought us out from there in order to bring us in," Deuteronomy 6:23

The story of the deliverance of the children of Israel from the land of Egypt is a profound metaphor concerning the walk of the average Christian. The goal of the children of Israel was to be delivered from the bondage of Egypt. The goal of God was to bring them into the Land of Canaan, (The place of God's promised inheritance.) That generation did not enter in to possess the Land of Canaan due to unbelief. Hebrews 3:19. Deliverance from Egypt was not an end in itself, it was a necessary means to an end.

What if during the entire time Israel was in bondage in Egypt they kept telling their kids and family about entering into the land of Canaan. Year after year all that the families heard was we're going to leave Egypt and enter into the land of Canaan. It would have made a difference in their expectations, and would have given them the courage to enter into the land of Canaan when the time came. Instead all they could talk about year after miserable year was their deliverance from the bondage of Egypt. When they came to the land of Canaan they were afraid to enter due to unbelief. They had the bondage attitude while in Egypt, and they still had the bondage attitude when God told them to go in and possess the land. What do you think would have happened if they spent their time talking about entering into the land of Canaan during all those years of captivity? They would have been prepared, in their hearts, to enter the land at any cost. They had their eyes on the wrong goal. Many people come to the Lord because they want deliverance from the bondage they are in, yet they do not want to enter the place of God's promised inheritance, so they wander in the desert. They had to wander in the wilderness for 40 years because of their unbelief. The time even came when they longed to be back in Egypt where they could eat leek and garlic. Numbers 11:5

It was God's will for them to go from Egypt directly into Canaan, not wander in the wilderness for 40 years. In the same way our focus needs to be adjusted so that we do not simply look at our salvation, *deliverance from Egypt*, as good as it is, but we need to look at the goal as to why God saved us. We need to enter into the place of God's promised inheritance.

To many Christians, the Christian life is nothing more than one long struggle, experiencing defeat after defeat. They have accepted the sacrifice of Jesus Christ the Lamb of God as the payment for their sins and, because of this, they know they will go to heaven when they die. Every day is nothing more than a constant battle; they try to do what's right and fail, but they know they will go to heaven when they die. They have a constant battle with sin and temptation. They so badly seek the love for others that they so desperately need, and fail time after time, but they know they will go to heaven when they die. If this sounds like you, congratulations, you are going to go to heaven when you die. But wait; there is more to the Christian life than simply going to heaven when you die. Because of the victory that we have in Christ, right now, here on earth, going to heaven when you die is a very nice addition, but it is not the essence of the Christian life. On Sundays, when you go to church, you hear such high-sounding words as, salvation, justification, sanctification, righteousness, deliverance, eternal life, redemption, regeneration and reconciliation. Although these are religious sounding words they mean more than simply religion. I've found that if there was no promise of heaven when I die, I would still want to live the Christian life here on earth. Once we discover the true meaning of what Christ accomplished on the cross we can live the life He intended us to live, the life of Christ in us. Through Him we can walk in the manifestation of the presence of God in our lives every day.

When, as a Christian, your primary goal is simply to get out of hell and into heaven it seems your vision is much too small. If that were the only goal, He would take us out of this world and into heaven the moment we were born again. He saved us not to simply get us into heaven when we die. It is not His goal that we wander in the wilderness until we get there. Nobody was ever designed to find fulfillment in life and all that God wants to give them in the wilderness. The wilderness was not a place of dwelling, but a desolate place to pass through on your way to the land of Canaan, the place of God's promised inheritance.

As we walk in His presence daily we find the Christian walk is a privilege not a burden. It's an adventure not something to endure until we get to heaven. If there were no promise of heaven when I die, I would still want to live in Christ every day, in His Presence. In His glory there is fullness of joy.

In his book, *The Saving Life of Christ*, Major W. Ian Thomas said, "There is nothing quite as boring as being religious, but there is nothing more exciting than being a Christian." [4]

Exodus 6: 6-8 gives seven steps the Children of Israel went through. It also shows where we are as a nation.

"Say therefore, to the sons of Israel, I am the Lord, and;
1. I will bring you out from under the burdens of the Egyptians,
2. And I will deliver you from their bondage.
3. I will also redeem you with an outstretched arm and with great judgments.
4. Then I will take you for My people, and I will be your God;
5. And you shall know that I am the Lord your God, who brought you out from under the burdens of the Egyptians.

6. And I will bring you to the land which I swore to give to Abraham, Isaac, and Jacob,
7. And I will give it to you for a possession; I am the Lord."

If I were to tell you that I live in Colorado Springs, you automatically know that certain things are true. You know that I live in the state of Colorado, I pay my taxes there, and I may enjoy the blessings that come with being a resident of Colorado. I could live in any other town in Colorado, and those general blessings would still be mine. Just because I live in Colorado doesn't mean I automatically live in Colorado Springs. But if I live in Colorado Springs you know that I automatically live in Colorado.

We can use this as an illustration of the Christian life. When you were born again you were saved from the penalty of your sin and you were placed into the Kingdom of God. That is the picture of Colorado. But if my goal is to live in Colorado Springs, the place of my promised inheritance, I could spend a lifetime wandering throughout the state of Colorado and never get to Colorado Springs. As a resident of Colorado, I have the right to live there if I want to, but it doesn't automatically happen.

I could talk about living in Colorado Springs, read all about it and dream about living there. I could go to lectures and hear others explain how nice it would be to live in Colorado Springs, but it would not make it so. Until I actually packed up and moved there, it would remain just a dream. The same is true when speaking of living in the place of God's promised inheritance. I could hear about it, read about it and dream about it; but it would not make it so. The only way of entering into the place of God's promised inheritance is by faith. The word of God shows us what Jesus did for us, so He could live His life in us, to make a way for us to walk in our promised inheritance.

As the Children of Israel were to enter into the place of God's promised inheritance by faith, so we too are to enter into the place of God's promised inheritance by faith. The Revival has begun; no longer are we to pray that the revival will come, but declare that it is here. As we fight the battle with the weapons of praise and worship, we are to continue to declare the victory through praise and worship. The weapons of our warfare have not changed.

GLORIFIED

John 7:37-39 says, "If any man is thirsty, let him come to Me and drink. He who believes in Me, as the Scripture said, from his innermost being shall flow rivers of living water. But this He spoke of the Spirit, whom those who believed in Him were to receive, *for the Spirit was not yet given, because Jesus was not yet glorified.*"

What was the prerequisite before the Holy Spirit could be poured out? What had to happen? The Holy Spirit could not be poured out until Jesus was glorified. When did this happen?

> "He commanded them not to leave Jerusalem, but to wait for what the Father had promised, which, He said, you heard of from Me; for John baptized with water, but you shall be baptized with the Holy Spirit, not many days from now." Acts 1:4-5

> "But when *He*, the Spirit of truth, comes, *He* will guide you into all the truth; for *He* will not speak on *His* own initiative, but whatever *He* hears, *He* will speak; and *He* will disclose to you what is to come. *He shall glorify Me; for He shall take of Mine, and shall disclose it to you.*" John 16:13-14

In the Old Testament when a man sinned he would take a sacrifice without spot or blemish, as a substitute for his sins. The Priest would then inspect the lamb or dove or whatever the sacrifice would be. The priest would not waste his time inspecting the man. *If the lamb was accepted the man was accepted.* Jesus, the Lamb of God that takes away the sin of the world, is our sacrifice for sin. When we come to the Father with our sacrifice: *The Lamb is accepted, therefore, the man is accepted.*

Proof that Jesus was glorified was the outpouring of the Holy Spirit on the day of Pentecost. The Holy Spirit could not be poured out until Jesus was glorified. Peter understood this in Acts 3:12-13 when the lame man was healed, "Men of Israel, why do you marvel at this, or why do you gaze at us, as if by our own power or piety we had made him walk? The God of Abraham, Isaac, and Jacob, the God of our fathers, has glorified His Servant Jesus." What was the prerequisite for healing? *Jesus was glorified.*

Many of us have witnessed hundreds and hundreds of healings and miracles. How can the lame walk? How can the blind see? How can the poor have the gospel preached to them? How can all this happen today? Because Jesus was glorified. The sacrifice was accepted by the Father. The price has been paid. Jesus, as the perfect sacrifice, was allowed back into the presence of the Father and received back into the glory that He had before the foundation of the world.

GLORY IN YOU
"Christ in you, the hope of glory." Colossians 1:27

In the upper room, after His farewell discourse Jesus prayed, and part of His prayer in John 17:22-23 He prayed: "The glory which You have given Me I have given to them, that they may be one, just as We are one; I in them and You in Me, that they may be perfected in unity, so that the world may know that You sent Me, and loved them, even as You have loved Me." The manifestation of the presence of God in you is His glory in you. When you received Jesus Christ as your savior and Lord His Holy Spirit came to dwell in you. He is the presence of God in you.

When you find a house you want to buy, you tell the realtor, "I want to buy that house." The realtor says, "You need to give me 20 percent down, earnest money." Earnest money is proof that you are serious, and you are obligated to buy that house.

It is proof and a token that there is more to come, and he can close the deal.

Ephesians 1:13 says:

"In Him, you also, after listening to the message of truth. The gospel of your salvation — having also believed, you were sealed in Him with the Holy Spirit of promise."

The Amplified Bible goes on and says:

"The (Spirit) is the guarantee of our inheritance — the first fruit, the pledge and foretaste, the down payment on our heritage — in anticipation of its full redemption and our acquiring (complete) possession of it, to the praise of His glory."

And again in 2 Corinthians 1:21-22:

"Now He who establishes us with you in Christ and anointed us is God, who also sealed us and gave us His Spirit in our hearts as a pledge," (down payment.)

"He has delivered us from the domain of darkness and has transferred us to the kingdom of His beloved Son." Colossians 1:13 KJV

"And it was for this He called you through our gospel, that you may gain the Glory of our Lord Jesus Christ." 2 Thessalonians 2:14

YOU WANT PROOF? He has given us His Spirit as a down payment.

When Adam sinned, we fell short of the Glory of God. Romans 3:23 Christ came to restore the Glory that was lost, and this will be culminated when we get home, but for now He has given us a down payment, earnest money, "Which is Christ in you, the hope of Glory. And we proclaim Him, admonishing every man and teaching every man with all wisdom, that we may present every man complete in Christ. And for this purpose also I labor, striving according to His power, which mightily works within me." Colossians 1:27-29

What is it we are hoping for, our HOPE? The answer is Glory, (the Divine manifestation of the presence of God). Where do we get this Glory? In Christ—Christ in you! We're not home yet, we're just passing through on our way home. In the meantime:

"... all of us, as with unveiled face, (because we) continued to behold (in the Word of God) as in a mirror the glory of the Lord, are constantly being transfigured into His very own image in ever increasing splendor and from one degree of glory to another; (for this comes) from the Lord (Who is) the Spirit." 2 Corinthians 3:18 Amplified Bible

"This mystery which has been hidden from the past ages and generations; but has now been manifested to His saints, to whom God willed to make known what is the riches of the glory of this mystery among the gentiles, which is Christ in you, the hope of Glory." Colossians 1:26-27

"For it was fitting for Him, for Whom are all things, and through Him are all things, in bringing many sons to glory." Hebrews 2:10

This hope, which means, anticipation and expectation, causes us to stand on tip-toes as we eagerly wait to see what God is going to do next. What blessing does He have in store for us today, what about tomorrow, and the next day? With Christ in us all things are possible.

In Ephesians 3:19 Paul prayed, "...and to know the love of Christ which surpasses knowledge, that you may be filled up to all the fullness of God." You and the church are the body of believers that is filled with the presence, power, agency and fullness of the riches of God and of Christ.

> "But we all, with unveiled face, beholding as in a mirror the glory of the Lord, are being transformed into the same image from glory to glory, just as from the Lord, the Spirit." 2 Corinthians 3:18

This is not a matter of us trying to get more of God, it is a matter of God getting more of us. Nowhere in the Bible does it say that we need to try harder; but it does say that we need to die daily and allow Jesus Christ to live His life in and through us. Not try, but trust. If you're trying hard to live the Christian life, cut it out, He never asked you to. He has asked you to allow Him to live His life through you.

> "Take My yoke upon you and learn from Me, for I am gentle and humble in heart, and you will find rest for your souls. For My yoke is easy and My burden is light." Matthew 11:29-30

He came to give us life and this life is in Him.

> "For God so loved the world, that He gave His only begotten Son, that whoever believes *in Him* shall not perish, but have eternal life. For God did not send the Son into the world to judge the world, but that the world might be saved *through Him*." John 3:16-17

In Him we have eternal life, the emphasis should be on *in Him*, but we often times put the emphasis on our believing. If it were up to our trying hard to believe then all the glory would go to us. The glory is His when this life is in and through Him.

> "By this the love of God was manifested in us, that God has sent His only begotten Son into the world so that we might live through Him." 1 John 4:9

> "Now to Him who is able to do far more abundantly beyond all that we ask or think, according to the

power that works within us to Him *be* the glory in the church and in Christ Jesus to all generations forever and ever." Ephesians 3:20-21

FOR THINE IS THE KINGDOM,
AND THE POWER, AND THE GLORY,
FOREVER. Amen

Appendix

Prayers by John Hayes

Who is John Hayes?

John Hayes is a Christian brother whom I had the privilege of ministering to when he started coming to our church. John was very poor and was thought of as being homeless. When he re-dedicated his life to the Lord I had the honor of baptizing him in our church. When he was baptized he wanted to wear his old clothes which he threw away after being baptized. He bought new clothes to be worn after he was baptized to show his new life in Christ.

John worked at a storage lot on El Paso Blvd and was allowed to stay in an apartment they provided for him as part of his pay. One night he heard some noise in the storage lot and confronted two men who were breaking into the storage units. They beat him to the point of death and he was found by a friend the next morning. He was taken to Penrose Hospital and put in ICU. I was called to the hospital and when I went to where he was I did not recognize him, he was beaten so badly. All he could do was to pray for those who had beaten him. Through this ordeal he lost one eye and has a few scars. Two years ago, he was evicted from his apartment when the storage facility was sold and now lives at a Christian Camp in Spokane. He just turned 80 years old and is about to lose his other eye due to the damage done in the beating.

When he came to the Lord he was given the ministry of writing gospel tracts, ministering to the homeless, and prayer. I asked him to write a few prayers to be used in my book. I'm honoring him by including many of those prayers in my book.

REFERENCES

Section 1

1. Zodhiates, Spiros. June 1992. *The Complete Word Study Dictionary*. AMG International, INC. Chattanooga, TN. AMG Publishers. 478.
2. Barnhouse, Donald Gray. 1959. *Romans Volume II, God's Remedy*. Grand Rapids, MI. William B. Eerdmans Publishing Company. 2:83.
3. Barnhouse, Donald Gray. 1959. *Romans Volume II, God's Remedy*. Grand Rapids, MI. William B. Eerdmans Publishing Company. 84.
4. Cahn, Johnathan. Copyright 2011 *The Harbinger*. Lake Mary, Florida, Charisma House Book Group 222.

Section 3

1. The Iverson Associates. 1971. *The New Testament and Wycliffe Bible Commentary*. New York, New York, Iverson Associates. 780.
2. Nee, Watchman. 1988. *Back to the Cross*. New York. New York Christian Fellowship Publishers. 1-2.
3. Zodhiates, Spiros. June 1992. *The Complete Word Study Dictionary*. AMG International, INC. Chattanooga, TN.. AMG Publishers.
4. Barnhouse, Donald Grey. 1959. *Romans Volume III, Victory with Christ*, Grand Rapids, Michigan, Wm. B. Eerdmans Publishing Company, 90.

5. Barnhouse, Donald Grey. 1959. *Romans Volume III, Victory with Christ*, Grand Rapids, MI. Wm. B. Eerdmans Publishing Company, 91.
6. Barnhouse, Donald Grey. 1959. *Romans Volume III, Victory with Christ*, Grand Rapids, MI. Wm. B. Eerdmans Publishing Company, 91.
7. Barnhouse, Donald Grey. 1959. *Romans Volume III, God's Freedom*. Grand Rapids, MI. Wm. B. Eerdmans Publishing Company, 65.
8. Barnhouse, Donald Grey. 1959. *Romans Volume III*. Grand Rapids, MI. Wm. B. Eerdmans Publishing Company.
9. Luther, Martin. 1967. *Luther's Large Catechism*. Minneapolis, MN. Augsburg Publishing House. 79-87.
10. Barnhouse, Donald Grey. 1959. *Romans Volume III, God's Freedom*. Grand Rapids, MI. Wm. B. Eerdmans Publishing Company. 68.
11. The Iverson Associates 1971, *The New Testament and Wycliffe Bible Commentary*. New York, NY. Iverson Associates 780.

Section 4

1. Duewal, Wesley, Orr, J. Edwin, 1989, *The Great Awakening of 1857-1858*, Wheaton, IL. www.smithworks.org/revival/1857.html.
2. Orr, J. Edwin. 1989. *The Great Awakening of 1857-1858*. Wheaton, IL. www.smithworks.org/revival/1857.html.

Section 5

1. Zhenying, Liu as told to Paul Hattaway. 2002. *The Heavenly Man*. Grand Rapids, MI. Kregel Publications.

Section 6

1. Hart, Benjamin. 1997. *Faith and Freedom*. Springfield, VA. *Christian Defense Fund*. 87.

2. Barton, David. *One Nation Under God*. http://www. WallBuilders.com
3. Hart, Benjamin. 1997. *Faith and Freedom. Springfield, VA. Christian Defense Fund.*
4. Thomas, Major W. Ian. 1978. *The Saving Life of Christ*. Grand Rapids, Michigan, Zondervan Publishing House.

BIBLIOGRAPHY

Scripture quotations taken from *The New American Standard Bible*. 1960, 1962, 1963, 1968, 1971, 1972, 1971, 1975, 1977, 1995. The Lochman Foundation. Used by permission. www.Lockman.org

Scripture quotations taken from *The Amplified Bible*. 1954, 1958, 1962, 1964, 1965, 1987. The Lockman Foundation. Used by permission. www.Lockman.org

Zodhiates, Th.D., Spiros. 1992. *The Complete Word Study Dictionary New Testament*. AMG International, Inc. D/B/A AMG Publishers

Barnhouse, Donald Grey. 1959. *Romans Volume 3, God's Grace, God's Freedom, God's Heirs*. Grand Rapids, MI. Philadelphia, PA. William B. Eerdmans Publishing Company. The Evangelical Foundation, Inc.

Barnhouse, Donald Grey. 1959. *Romans Volume II, God's Remedy*. Grand Rapids, MI. Philadelphia, PA. William B. Eerdmans Publishing Company. The Evangelical Foundation, Inc.

Hart, Benjamin. 1997. *Faith and Freedom*. Springfield, VA. Christian Defense Fund

Stanford, Miles J. 1982. *Principles of Spiritual Growth, The Green Letters*. Lincoln, NB. Back to the Bible.

Nee, Watchman. 1988. *Back To The Cross*. 1988. New York, NY. New York Christian Fellowship.

Cahn, Johnathan. 2011. *The Harbinger*. Lake Mary, FL. Charisma House Book Group,

The Iverson Associates. 1971. *The New Testament and Wycliffe Bible Commentary*. New York, NY. Iverson Associates.

Luther, Martin. 1967, *Luther's Large Catechism,* Minneapolis, MN. Augsburg Publishing House

Orr, J. Edwin. 1989. *The Great Awakening of 1857-1858*. Wheaton, IL. www.smithworks.org/revival/1857.html

Zhenying, Liu, as told to Paul Hattaway. 2002. *The Heavenly Man*. Grand Rapids, MI. Kregel Publications

Thomas, Major W. Ian. 1978. *The Saving Life of Christ*. Grand Rapids, MI. Zondervan Publishing House.

Barton, David. *One Nation Under God*. www.wallbuilders.com

ENDORSEMENTS

Wally Dallenbach: "I had time to review your book *The Glory of Man*. I'm impressed with the explanatory information that you have brought forth out of the Bible about God's Word and love. You have simplified the word for a young Christian, or a person that is searching to be a Christian, or a person not yet a Christian, and a person asking, "Why do I want to be a Christian?"

The reward is Heaven and good deeds do not get it done. Your book is not only a guide but a study that can help to make it happen. May God Bless you for your conviction to guide others to the checkered flag in Heaven."

Chuck Chambers from Florida writes: "I have read your book *The Glory of Man* three different times. On each reading I get more out of what you have written. I also have picked it up and read various portions as something you said came to my mind. Your book is a great blessing in my life and I will read it again."

"*The Glory of Man* is a book I want to give to all my friends. It is riveting, exciting, and full of solid scripture to support every word. I wanted to highlight every other sentence and ponder it all, praying for the ongoing of God's amazing work and glory. You'll want to read and worship and praise Him over and over. This is a MUST-read giving God honor and glory.

Gratefully in Jesus! **Darlene Poirson** - Manitou Springs, CO.

P.S. As a Bible Study Fellowship teacher for 22 years I keep appreciating God's Word foremost. You certainly upheld that tremendously. Thank You!"

"In reading *The Glory of Man*, with each word being brought out, a new revelation comes. It's about the glory of God from start to finish. It brought tears to my eyes reading about the Glory of God. Thanks brother David for bringing new insight to God's word. Without the anointing of God on you, you could not have written this master letter. Good Book!" **Pastor James Saunders**, Colorado Springs, CO.

"I am proud of your accomplishments both in the stories you share and in completing this book. Christ has filled you to overflowing and I am glad you are bold enough to share your blessings from Jesus." Love, **Brother Allen**, Canon City, CO.

"What I have genuinely appreciated about my reading of *The Glory of Man* is the emphasis on Identity. As I have recently retired from the US Army, I've had to confront myself as I tried to learn how I fit into the world now that a part of my life is complete. Some of the vital principles David Bachoroski expressed helped me understand where my true identity resides, in Jesus. The reality of this concept gives me confidence that my life in Him is more relevant, and yes, still exciting." **Sgt. 1st Class Gary M. Stacy, USAR, Retired**.

The Glory of Man is a timely writing that reminds us of something that the modern Christian seems to forget all too easily. We are not alone, and God has not forgotten us. As Christians we are here for a purpose that is powerful and wonderfully awesome. We are living, walking, and powerful praise and prayer warriors, carrying forth the good news that eternal life begins now, and we should live our lives accordingly." **Pastor Mark Baker**, Colorado Springs, CO.

Billy Joe Patton writes, "I am really, really enjoying your book David. It is one of those where you start to highlight stuff and if you did you would highlight the whole thing!"

ABOUT THE AUTHOR

David Bachoroski

David Bachoroski is retired from General Motors Corporation where he tested cars on Pikes Peak for 33 years. He is currently Chairman of the Pikes Peak Hill Climb Historical Association. an office that he has held for 10 years.

After thirty-three years of automobile testing with the General Motors Proving Ground, David retired in 1998. He was Manager of the GM Pikes Peak Vehicle Test Headquarters in Manitou Springs, Colorado and has completed over five thousand round trips to the Summit of Pikes Peak, touted as the world's highest highway at 14,110 feet.

Twelve times he was the Pikes Peak Hill Climb Pace Car Driver. He also built and prepared pace cars for such notables as Elke Summers, Rick Mears, Johnny Parsons, Sr., Al Unser, Jr. and Louis Unser. Ten times he was Pikes Peak Hill Climb car owner and builder with driver Jerry King, and assisted race crews with such notables as Bobby Unser, Sr., Robbie Unser, Bobby Unser, Jr., Larry Ragland and brothers Frank and Nick Sanborn.

He also served two terms on the City of Colorado Springs Pikes Peak Highway Advisory Commission. He assisted Mankato State University with a Guiness World Record of first solar car to the Summit of Pikes Peak in 1990 and was founder and organizer of the 1992 Pikes Peak Solar/Electric Challenge, in which he worked with colleges and universities throughout the country.

He was nominated for Who's Who of Business Leaders in 1993 and was the subject of numerous articles in the Colorado Car Book, author Bud Wells, Race to the Clouds, author Stan

Degeer, Denver Post, Rocky Mountain News, Gazette Telegraph and Pikes Peak Journal.

Bachoroski attended Adams State College in Alamosa, Colorado, where he majored in Business and music and has a Business Degree from Blair Business College, and an Automobile Mechanics Degree from Commercial Trades Institute.

He lives in Colorado Springs, CO, with his wife Connie, and has two daughters living near them, Stephanie and Michelle. Hobbies include, guitar playing, teaching and writing. He is also a member of the First Evangelical Free Church where he has held many offices since 1974. He and his wife became born again Christians in 1972. David went through a period of three years where he could read nothing but God's Word; no newspapers, magazines or television. He needed the cleansing power of God's Word up to twenty hours a day. He learned that; "you shall know the truth and the truth shall set you free." This could be called his personal Bible School. After that he has taught at numerous Bible Studies, and led many prayer groups for over 40 years, and has seen many lives changed.

BOOKS BY DAVID BACHOROSKI

Healing and the Prayer of Faith
By David Bachoroski

In this in-depth Bible study, David draws on both the Old and New Testaments with an emphasis on the healing of spirit, soul, and body.

Many believe that sickness is just their lot in life, an affliction that must be endured. David shows God's desire to heal us, the finished work of the cross of Christ as it relates to healing, and the need for the manifest presence of the Glory of God in our prayers. This book is a faith-builder and provides a strong biblical basis for not just our own healing, but ministering healing to others.

"And the prayer of faith shall save the sick, and the Lord shall raise him up." James 5:15

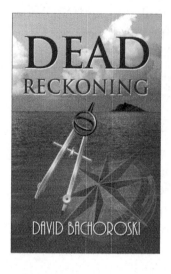

Dead Reckoning
By David Bachoroski

Why can't I do what is right? Many of us have asked this very question. We have tried to overcome our fleshly desires by self-determination, will power, joining focus groups, accountability groups, and 12 Step programs. David expounds on the power of Jesus to overcome addictions, thought patterns, and harmful habits in this short book, *Dead Reckoning.*

"Likewise reckon ye also yourselves to be dead indeed unto sin, but alive unto God through Jesus Christ our Lord." Romans 6:11

The only one who is capable of living the Christian life is Jesus Christ himself. He never asked us to lead this life by our own ability and by trying harder. He came to live his life *through* us. David shows how to overcome guilt, fear, condemnation, and how to appropriate the life of Christ in us, so that we may live the overcoming life God intended for us.

Flowing Streams Books
See our complete catalog and visit us online at
www.flowingstreamsbooks.com

Made in the USA
Middletown, DE
05 March 2019